CONTENTS

MAPS

STATISTICAL TABLES

POTTERY ILLUSTRATIONS

Figures

PREFACE

More than one ton of pottery was recovered during ten years of rescue excavations in the Castle Street area of Plymouth. Other finds from the sites include a range of marked clay pipes, already published (Barber and Oswald, 1969); and metalwork and glass which will be the subject of a future publication.

For this report the pottery from all the Castle Street sites has been treated as one unstratified group, as the excavations were on the site of the town's communal refuse tip and stratigraphical relationships were poor. The problems and nature of the excavation are explained in the Introduction (p 1). The tin-glazed wares, with the exception of those from Montelupo, Italy and copperlustre ware from Spain, are still being studied and regrettably cannot be included here. The approximate quantities of tin-glazed pottery are noted in the section on quantification (p 2).

The report which follows is the work of a number of experts and we are most grateful to them all for their interest and advice freely given over a number of years. The sections relating to the British coarse wares are the joint work of R Coleman-Smith and T Pearson, with drawings by R Coleman-Smith. The sections on the imported pottery are the work of Ann Clark, advised by J G Hurst and financed by the Department of the Environment. The drawings of the imported pottery were prepared in the DoE drawing office by C Bonnington, S Heaser and J Thorne. J Ayers and M Archer of the Victoria and Albert Museum kindly provided advice. Mrs A Preston has given much practical and editorial assistance in Plymouth. Many volunteers have also helped with this project and we would like to express our thanks to them all.

CYNTHIA GASKELL BROWN
December 1978

ACKNOWLEDGEMENTS

Map 1 prepared and drawn by J Barber. Maps 2–5 compiled by R Coleman-Smith (based on information from A Clark; Charleston, 1968; Caiger-Smith, 1973; Cooper, 1972; and Steinzeug. Museum for Arts and Crafts, Koln, 1971). We are grateful to Mrs G Bainbridge, University of Newcastle-on-Tyne, for assistance with the graphics on maps 2–5.

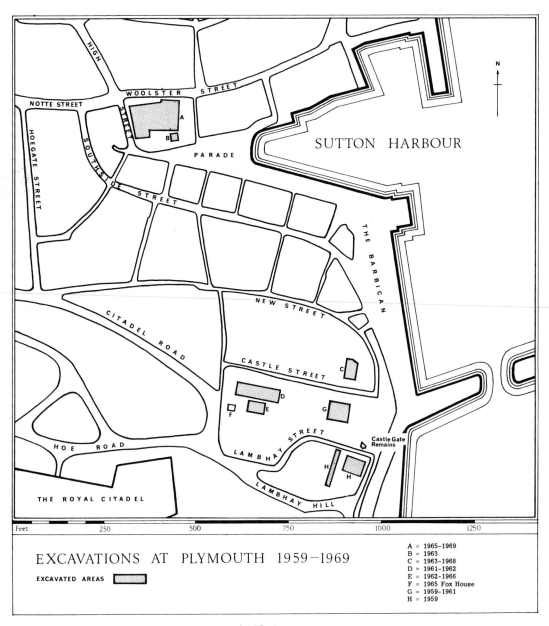

EXCAVATIONS AT PLYMOUTH 1959–1969

EXCAVATED AREAS

A = 1965-1969
B = 1963
C = 1963-1968
D = 1961-1962
E = 1962-1966
F = 1965 Fox House
G = 1959-1961
H = 1959

MAP 1

INTRODUCTION

The pottery catalogued and discussed in this monograph was found during excavations conducted between 1959 and 1969 on sites in the vicinity of the old harbour of Plymouth, Sutton Pool, and comes from sites C, D, E, G and H (Map 1).

Early in 1959 an extensive programme of demolition, preparatory to the erection of Corporation housing, cleared an area at Castle Street and Lambhay Street (SX/48255395: see Map 1) known to have been the site of a castle built late in the 14th century to command the narrow entrance to Sutton Pool. Little was known of the exact size and lay-out of the castle, of which only a small tower, one of a pair flanking an entrance, now remains above ground. The building had been slighted in the 1660s, when Charles II's Royal Citadel was erected nearby at the south-east extremity of Plymouth Hoe, and though substantial medieval remains survived into the 19th century, they were removed without record in the 1880s and 1890s. In the hope of learning more about the castle prior to the redevelopment of its site, an excavation was sponsored jointly by the then Ministry of Works and Plymouth Corporation, and directed by Miss V B Ledger, MA, Archaeological Assistant at Plymouth City Museum and Art Gallery.

No trace of the castle was revealed in the excavation, and at the time the great quantity of post-medieval potsherds and other artifacts found in the trenches seemed inadequate compensation for the structural remains which had been expected. Only when the present writer had succeeded to Miss Ledger's position in 1960 did examination of the Castle Street finds, by Mrs J Minter and subsequently by Mr J G Hurst, reveal their true significance as one of the most comprehensive collections of native and imported post-medieval pottery types to have been recovered, up to that time, from excavations in the United Kingdom. The foundation trenches dug for the new block of flats on the south side of Castle Street were now closely observed, specifically with a view to locating and recovering further significant post-medieval deposits, as well as to continuing the fruitless quest for the castle foundations. In May, 1961, a further short excavation, directed by Mrs Minter for the Ministry of Works, explored an area immediately east of Cooksley's Court (part of Area G on Map 1),

while further work west of it was undertaken throughout 1961 and 1962 by members of Plymouth City Museum Archaeology Group and other volunteers under the writer's supervision. It was at this point that the presence of many marked clay tobacco pipes among the finds began to be noticed, and a particularly careful watch was kept for further examples. Between 1963 and 1968 the writer directed the excavation by voluntary labour of the rear portions of two contiguous tenements on the north side of Castle Street (nos 25 and 26), the systematic exploration of a limited area (some 50 feet by 25 feet) proving most rewarding in terms of complete pottery profiles as well as in clay pipes and other small finds.

The post-medieval deposits at Castle Street are not associated with contemporary structures, but represent accumulations of domestic refuse collected by communal effort and tipped in an area of several acres over a considerable period of time. Up to the mid-17th century, tipping must have taken place chiefly on the waste ground between the castle and the built-up area (represented at that time by New Street and the Barbican), while after about 1660 the site of the castle itself was available, first, for quarrying the walls and the limestone bedrock beneath them, then for tipping, and finally, about the middle of the 18th century, for building. The late 18th-century and 19th-century deposits at Castle Street are smaller in quantity, representing the refuse disposal of households in the immediate neighbourhood, as opposed to the large-scale disposal of the whole town's garbage which seems to have prevailed in the preceding centuries.

The 16th- and 17th-century deposits on the south side of Castle Street had been much disturbed by later foundation trenches, and were excavated at speed, in co-operation with the contractors' schedules. They exhibited little stratification, and produced no strictly closed groups from drains, wells, or cess-pits.

The limited excavation of the north side of Castle Street was undertaken at greater leisure, without the immediate threat of building activity, and the early deposits were found largely undisturbed. A lower layer of brown clay, possibly in the first instance removed as overburden from limestone required for quarrying nearby, and varying in depth from one to three feet, was found spread over the entire excavated area, resting on an almost sterile orange clay layer immediately above the limestone bedrock. The brown clay layer, though again not strictly a sealed deposit, being covered only by a thicker layer of black soil from two to six feet deep with predominantly mid-17th century artifacts at its base and late 18th-century ones at the top, produced, none the less, a remarkably homogenous assemblage of finds of late 16th and early 17th character. Of particular interest was the variety of the imported pottery which included German stoneware from Siegburg and Frechen, and slipware from Wanfried and Weser; South-West French green-glazed and polychrome earthenware and Beauvais sgraffito earthenware; Netherlands maiolica; North Italian marbled ware and Montelupo-style maiolica; Spanish tin-glazed earthenware and lustre ware, red micaceous earthenware and olive jars; Ming porcelain and Swatow enamelled earthenware from the Far East.

Within this brown clay layer was found, in 1964, a small deposit of darker soil (representing perhaps an individual basketful of rubbish) containing the greater part of a Netherlands maiolica platter with polychrome decoration, several sherds of a Ming porcelain cup with blue and white decoration, a glass flask, and a group of pipes discussed in Barber and Oswald (1969).

Further light on the pattern of Plymouth's trade with the Netherlands and the Iberian Peninsula during the 17th and early 18th centuries will be forthcoming when the delftwares among the Castle Street finds are published. Continental and English wares are present; their dating and relative proportions at different periods are estimated in this report (see p 2, 3).

METHOD OF ANALYSIS AND QUANTIFICATION

The pottery was sorted into types by country and forms within each type. From this analysis the numbers of sherds and an estimated minimum number of vessels was recorded for each form of each type. The large size and varied composition of this assemblage gave rise to problems in identification, terminology, and in the assessment of quantity. The wide range of forms, sizes and decoration (or lack of it) of the material led to discrepancies in the estimation of the minimum numbers of vessels. It was easier to give an accurate assessment of decorated sherds. In cases where joins occurred, or where it was clear that sherds were from one vessel they have been counted as one vessel. With plain wares, however, sherds from the same vessel may have been overlooked. The number of rims, bases and body sherds has been noted.

The large number, 51,146 sherds, of the British coarse wares meant that strict sorting to identify individual vessels could not be carried out. In many cases it was not possible to identify the form of the vessel from the body sherds alone, and these have been classed under the group of forms from which they most probably derived. A minimum assessment of the number of vessels was, therefore, based on the number of rim sherds which did not fit together. Where the class was sufficiently distinctive or decorated a more reliable estimate has been given. The assemblage, which in itself was only a small sample of a potentially much greater deposit, has meant that many types were fragmentary, and in some cases there were no rim sherds. In this case the minimum number of vessels was calculated as the number of base sherds.

The quantities of each form of each type are stated in detail in the text and are shown in Tables 3–11. The totals of sherds and minimum vessels for each country are shown in the summary chart (Table 1).

The total figure of 57,700 sherds does not include the tin-glazed wares which are to be published separately. Estimated percentages of tin-glazed wares have been provided by L L Lipski (Table 2). The figures are not strictly compatible with the quantities expressed in Table 1a but an attempt has been made to incorporate them in Table 1b.

Tables 1a & b.   Total number of sherds and minimum number of vessels

COUNTRY	TOTALS (Without tin-glazed wares)				TOTALS (With tin-glazed wares)	
	NO. SHERDS	%	MIN. NO. VESSELS	%	MIN. NO. VESSELS (estimate)	%
TOTALS	57,700	100	9,572	100	11,072	100
BRITAIN	51,146	88·641	7,852	82·031	8,032	72·543
CHINA 17th century	103	0·179	43	0·449	43	0·388
CHINA 18th century	1,284	2·225	474	4·952	474	4·281
FAR EAST	1	0·002	1	0·010	1	0·009
FRANCE	572	0·991	126	0·316	129	1·165
GERMANY	2,027	3·513	363	3·792	393	3·549
ITALY	663	1·149	210	2·194	219	1·978
JAPAN	2	0·003	2	0·021	2	0·018
MIDDLE EAST	1	0·002	1	0·010	1	0·009
MEDITERRANEAN	41	0·071	—	—	—	—
NETHERLANDS	375	0·649	174	1·818	699	6·313
SPAIN	1,485	2·574	326	3·406	1,079	9·745
	1a				*1b*	

Table 2.   Estimated numbers of tin-glazed wares

COUNTRY	TIN GLAZES (estimates)			
	17th CENTURY %	NO. OF VESSELS	18th CENTURY %	NO. OF VESSELS
Spain and Portugal	50	750	0·2	3
Netherlands	33	495	2·0	30
Britain	4·0	60	8·0	120
Germany	2·0	30	—	—
Italy	0·1	1·5	0·5	7·5
France	0·2	3·0	—	—
TOTALS	89·3	1,340	10·7	160

Possible number of vessels represented = 1,500–2,000.
Percentages are good estimates, number of vessels less reliable.
For this table it has been assumed that 1,500 vessels are represented.

Table 3

BRITAIN

COARSEWARES

		Bottles	Bucket pots	Bowls	Chafing dishes	Cresset lamps	Candlesticks	Costrels	Chamber pots	Colanders	Chimney pots	Cisterns	Cups/mugs/tankards	Crocks/large jars	Press moulded dishes	Dishes	Baking dishes	Jars	Jugs
Donyatt 1500–1750	No. Sh.	3	13	1627	68			4	138	6		12	296	19		3781	22	101	279
	Min. No. V.	2	6	827	20			3	70	4		8	47	19		1534	11	76	142
Forest of Dean 1600–1700	No. Sh.												7						
	Min. No. V.												6						
Hampshire/Dorset 1700–1900	No. Sh.			12	17		3		6			1	490		11	27	116	1151	52
	Min. No. V.			10	15		2		6			1	250		4	21	45	201	40
Metropolitan Slipware 1600–1700	No. Sh.				2											20			
	Min. No. V.				1											16			
Midlands Purple 1600–1900	No. Sh.			239									16		85	33	1		
	Min. No. V.			45									10		68	30	1		
North Devon 1600 →	No. Sh.			137	50	9	1	8	150			23	24	19		678	19	878	415
	Min. No. V.			98	38	8	1	6	119			23	11	19		256	13	299	98
South-West Micaceous (St. Germans Type) 1500 →	No. Sh.	2		240	2	2	2				2	74					5	391	254
	Min. No. V.	2		158	2	2	2				2	67					4	76	235
Staffs./Bristol Manganese Glazed 1680–1750	No. Sh.												119						
	Min. No. V.												43						
Staffs. Red and Agate 1700–1750	No. Sh.			2															
	Min. No. V.			2															
Staffs./Bristol Yellow Slipware 1680–1750	No. Sh.			1744									320		546				
	Min. No. V.			532									155		230				
Sussex 1700–1800	No. Sh.			2														42	
	Min. No. V.			2														27	
Stonewares 1800–1900	No. Sh.																		
	Min. No. V.																		
Local Redwares 1800 →	No. Sh.										28								
	Min. No. V.										6								
Miscellaneous Post-medieval	No. Sh.																		
Miscellaneous medieval	No. Sh.																		

4

Table 3 (continued)

BRITAIN

COARSEWARES

		Jugs/jars/puncheons	Puzzle jugs	Jugs/cisterns (medieval)	Ladles	Lid	Ointment pot	Pans	Salting pans	Puncheons	Pedestal bases	Pilchard jars	Plates	Pipkins	Porringers	Ridge tiles	Spittoons	Watering cans	Miscellaneous sherds	Totals
Donyatt 1500–1750	No. Sh.	1662			5			12	19	216			8	58	1079				55	9464
	Min. No. V.	185			5			3	10	93			6	38	312					3411
Forest of Dean 1600–1700	No. Sh.																			7
	Min. No. V.																			6
Hampshire/Dorset 1700–1900	No. Sh.		1				12			24			5	17	203				666	2814
	Min. No. V.		1				12			19			2	14	78					721
Metropolitan Slipware 1600–1700	No. Sh.																		3	25
	Min. No. V.																		3	20
Midlands Purple 1600–1900	No. Sh.					1				64			1		102					542
	Min. No. V.					1				38			1		39					233
North Devon 1600 →	No. Sh.	15,600			1			9		486	2	820	63	38	104		1	3	5	19,543
	Min. No. V.				1			6		173	2	343	48	13	77		1	2		1646
South-West Micaceous (St. Germans Type) 1500 →	No. Sh.			13						202			2	18		45			8601	9857
	Min. No. V.			12						176			2	17		31				788
Staffs./Bristol Manganese Glazed 1680–1750	No. Sh.																			119
	Min. No. V.																			43
Staffs. Red and Agate 1700–1750	No. Sh.																		1	3
	Min. No. V.																		1	3
Staffs./Bristol Yellow Slipware 1680–1750	No. Sh.	2049																		7313
	Min. No. V.																			917
Sussex 1700–1800	No. Sh.							3		24									33	104
	Min. No. V.							3		13										45
Stonewares 1800–1900	No. Sh.																		128	128
	Min. No. V.																			
Local Redwares 1800 →	No. Sh.									76									138	242
	Min. No. V.									13										19
Miscellaneous Post-medieval	No. Sh.																		643	643
Miscellaneous medieval	No. Sh.																		342	342
Total Sherds Total minimum No. of Vessels																				51,146 7852

Table 4

CHINA 17th CENTURY PORCELAIN		Cups/bowls	Cups	Stem cups	Bowls	Large bowls	Small bowls	Plates	Totals
Type I 'Carrack'	No. Sh.	11						30	41
	Min. No. V.	4						3	7
Type II 'Transitional Period'	No. Sh.					7	6	11	24
	Min. No. V.					7	6	11	24
Type III 'Provincial Wares'	No. Sh.				4				4
	Min. No. V.				1				1
Type IV	No. Sh.	29							29
	Min. No. V.	7							7
Type V	No. Sh.		1						1
	Min. No. V.		1						1
Type VI 'Famille Verte'	No. Sh.				2				2
	Min. No. V.				1				1
Type VII	No. Sh.		1	1					2
	Min. No. V.		1	1					2
Totals	No. Sh.								103
	Min. No. V.								43

Table 5

CHINA 18th CENTURY PORCELAIN		Bowls	Fluted bowls	Shallow bowls	Hexagonal bowls	Cups	Mugs	Bowls/plates/dishes	Plates	Cylindrical jars	Miscellaneous	Totals
Type I Blue and white, dragon	No. Sh.	28							52			80
	Min. No. V.	23										23
Type II 'café au lait' brown glazed	No. Sh.					21						21
	Min. No. V.					9						9
Type III 'Chinese Imari'	No. Sh.	38	2			21		8				69
	Min. No. V.	33	2			12		8				55
Type IV enamelled porcelains	No. Sh.	15										15
	Min. No. V.	6										6
Type V	No. Sh.	1										1
	Min. No. V.	1										1
Type VI	No. Sh.								1			1
	Min. No. V.								1			1
Type VII	No. Sh.	132							21		696	849
	Min. No. V.	66							5		170	241
Type VIII 'Famille Rose'	No. Sh.	29	6	3		91	1	12	58	1	24	224
	Min. No. V.	22	6	3		39	1	1	58	1		131
Type IXa Swatow stoneware	No. Sh.	10										10
	Min. No. V.	2										2
Type IXb Swatow blue and white	No. Sh.	4							5			9
	Min. No. V.	1							2			3
Type IXc Swatow late 18thC.	No. Sh.	1							1			2
	Min. No. V.	1							1			2
Totals												1284
												474

Table 6

FRANCE		Dishes	Chafing dishes	Jugs	Flanged dishes	Bowls	Saintonge brown	Polychrome handles	Decorated knobs	Candlesticks	Figurine	Plates	Jars	Costrels	Type II Flasks	Miscellaneous	Totals
Beauvais Sgrafitto, single slip	No. Sh.	9															9
	Min. No. V.	3															3
Beauvais Sgrafitto, double slip	No. Sh.	10		1													11
	Min. No. V.	3		1													4
Martincamp Slipware	No. Sh.	6															6
	Min. No. V.	4															4
Saintonge, Green and Yellow	No. Sh.		139														139
	Min. No. V.																—
Saintonge, Late Polychrome	No. Sh.		10	7	4	33	1	16	2	1	1					17	90
	Min. No. V.			7	4	17	1										29
South West French	No. Sh.					6						14	2			212	234
	Min. No. V.					1						14	2			66	73
Beauvais Stoneware	No. Sh.			5									1	2		8	16
	Min. No. V.			1									1	1			3
Martincamp Stoneware	No. Sh.														14		14
	Min. No. V.																—
Normandy Stoneware	No. Sh.			6									3	1		40	50
	Min. No. V.			3									3	1			7
Miscellaneous	No. Sh.			1									1	1			3
	Min. No. V.			1									1	1			3
Totals	No. Sh.																572
	Min. No. V.																126

Table 7

GERMANY

		Bellarmines	Jugs	Cups	Mugs	Seltzer bottles	Tankards	Chamber pots	Handles	Spouts	Plates	Cups/bowls	Bowls	Pipkins	Acanthus	Miscellaneous	Totals
Niederrheinische Slipware	No. Sh.												2				2
	Min. No. V.												1				1
Cologne/Frechen	No. Sh.	858													22		880
	Min. No. V.	93															93
Langerwehe	No. Sh.		4	8												45	57
	Min. No. V.		4	1													5
Raeren	No. Sh.		106	21													127
	Min. No. V.		9	7													16
Raeren/Langerwehe	No. Sh.		19													13	32
	Min. No. V.		8														8
Siegburg	No. Sh.		5			4										19	28
	Min. No. V.		2														2
Westerwald	No. Sh.		257			3	4	32	35	5						219	556
	Min. No. V.		11				4	9								46	76
Wanfried	No. Sh.										94	16					110
	Min. No. V.										61	14					75
Weser	No. Sh.		5								219		9	2		1	236
	Min. No. V.		5								77		9	2			93
Totals	No. Sh.																2027
	Min. No. V.																363

8

Table 8

ITALY		Bowls	Deep bowls	Straight sided bowls	Cavalier pattern plates	Costrels	Carinated dishes	Dishes	Jugs	Pedestal bases	Miscellaneous	Totals
Montelupo	No. Sh.		70		8			142	12	4	45	**281**
	Min. No. V.		11		3			49	3	4	8	**78**
Faenza	No. Sh.										2	**2**
	Min. No. V.										2	**2**
Liguria	No. Sh.										1	**1**
	Min. No. V.										1	**1**
North Italian, marbled	No. Sh.	113		50	5	11	11					**290**
	Min. No. V.	84		7	5	2	11					**109**
North Italian, sgraffito	No. Sh.	26					12				51	**89**
	Min. No. V.	8					3				9	**20**
Totals	No. Sh.											**663**
	Min. No. V.											**210**

Table 9

NETHERLANDS		Colanders	Pipkins	Dishes	Bowls	Jars	Handles	Jugs/jars	Miscellaneous	Totals
Dutch Type, Brown	No. Sh.	32	22	11	2	4	4		3	**78**
	Min. No. V.	7	22	9	2	4			3	**47**
Dutch Type, Yellow	No. Sh.		1		33			28	62	**124**
	Min. No. V.		1		30			15		**46**
North Holland, Slipware	No. Sh.		2	5	166					**173**
	Min. No. V.		2	5	74					**81**
Totals	No. Sh.									**375**
	Min. No. V.									**174**

Table 10

SPAIN		Bowls	Costrels	Heavy flanged dishes	Jars	Olive jars	Jugs	Plates	Triangular rims	Miscellaneous	Totals
Green Glazed	No. Sh.			6							6
	Min. No. V.			5							5
Merida	No. Sh.	203	40	116	109		310		8	24	810
	Min. No. V.	154	21	43	25		4		8	6	261
Olive Jars	No. Sh.					566					566
	Min. No. V.					23					23
Starred Costrels	No. Sh.		41								41
	Min. No. V.		2								2
Copper Lustre	No. Sh.	43					19				62
	Min. No. V.	26					9				35
Totals	No. Sh.										1485
	Min. No. V.										326

Table 11

OTHER COUNTRIES		Plates	Bowls	Jars	Miscellaneous	Totals
Mediterranean	No. Sh.				41	41
	Min. No. V.				—	—
Middle East	No. Sh.		1			1
	Min. No. V.		1			1
Japan	No. Sh.	2				2
	Min. No. V.	2				2
Far East	No. Sh.			1		1
	Min. No. V.			1		1

DISCUSSION

THE BRITISH WARES

The date range represented by the material from Castle Street extends from the medieval period to the early 20th century, with the majority of sherds belonging to the late 17th century. As such, the quantities of sherds of different periods expressed in this assemblage probably only reflects a bias of the excavation, being only a small part of the material deposited on the site. This aspect is unquantifiable without further excavation. The original stratigraphic/trench sequence is lost, which in terms of the proportions and dates of the material excavated takes away much of its value. In this report, particularly for the British coarse wares, broad date ranges for each type have been given.

In the large group of British coarse wares, the Donyatt type wares can, at present, be the most tightly dated and identified from the excavations at the kiln sites (Coleman-Smith and Pearson, 1970, and forthcoming) and from excavations in Taunton (CRAAGS, forthcoming). This group of pottery has an overall date range from c1500–1750, with 13 sherds of the 16th century; 31 sherds of the early 17th century; 9,241 sherds of the late 17th century; and 179 sherds of early 18th-century date.

The North Devon pottery is, at present, difficult to date, as little material from sealed groups is available (or published), apart from the excavation of waste pottery from Barnstaple Castle (information from T Miles). The early 17th century origin of this slipware/sgraffito industry is not clear. For the purposes of this report, a chronological breakdown similar to the Donyatt material may be assumed.

The South West Micaceous wares (St German's-type wares) are important because they may reflect the late medieval 'local' ceramics in Plymouth. The majority of this pottery was of a medieval character and form, although some sherds would appear to show decorative techniques and styles reflected in 17th-century ceramics from elsewhere. If this is so, then a large proportion of the imported pottery was current with the St German's-type wares. In such a situation there may have been a demand for better quality (and cheaper?) pottery from the Donyatt and North Devon regions.

Further evidence of the movement of pottery into Plymouth may come from an examination of Port Books for the ports of Bristol, Bridgwater, Lyme Regis and Barnstaple. An example of this can be seen from the Bristol Port Books, Customs, Christmas 1780–Midsummer 1781, coastwise out (BRO E 190/1233/3). '1781, Jan 18. The Unity of Plymouth. Eight crates of earthenware from Bristol to Plymouth'. There are also references to stoneware being sent to Plymouth from Bristol (information from D Dawson). Stonewares were absent from the Castle Street assemblage, apart from some sherds of the late nineteenth century. They were either absent in Plymouth at the time, or have been removed for analysis and lost prior to the present work.

Within the large 17th-century group, the Donyatt wares included proportionately more decorated vessels than the North Devon group, the latter containing more of the larger coarse wares. These relationships can be seen in the chart for the British coarse wares (Table 3), and the detailed figures (pp 4 and 21).

THE IMPORTS

It is a great pity that, as described in the Introduction, the pottery found was badly stratified and mixed, for the deposit contains the largest groups so far found of most types. This means that the total assemblage cannot be adequately quantified due to the differing dates of the various types. In particular most of the imports, except the Westerwald and later tin-glazed wares and Chinese porcelain, date from the period 1550–1650 while the main bulk of the local wares are after 1650. Some of the local types thought to be later must date from before this as is suggested by recent evidence from the earliest settlements in Virginia. In the late 16th and early 17th century nevertheless the percentage of imports must be far greater than the overall figures, perhaps as much as fifty percent.

Of far greater significance, however, are the relative numbers of imports showing that the wide range of imports is by no means equally represented. This was not at all clear from the Southampton report where there was no attempt to quantify the finds (Platt and Coleman-Smith, 1975). Seventeenth century Chinese porcelain is surprisingly rare in view of contacts with the Netherlands and the vast quantities reaching North-West Europe. By the 18th century, though, with direct British trade there is a very considerable amount at a time when there were few other pottery imports because of the predominance of Staffordshire, and the fact that Britain was making its own tin-glazed wares and stonewares. Japanese, other South-East Asian, Middle Eastern and general Mediterranean wares are only represented by odd vessels which seem to have come in singly rather than by proper trade.

The two hundred Italian vessels show considerable increase over late medieval times when hardly any Italian pottery is found in North-West Europe. There is a large proportion of Montelupo tin-glazed ware, and about one and a half times as many lead-glazed marbled and sgraffito vessels from the Pisa area. These two centres seem to have specialised in and cornered the market for exports, the finer wares being hardly represented at all, except for a few from Liguria.

The Spanish and Portugese pottery, comprising more than one thousand vessels, surprisingly accounts for the largest group of imports. The finer lustre wares which predominate in the medieval period quickly fade out, to be replaced by the seven hundred and fifty mainly blue and white coarser wares, in the same way as the Italian maiolica is from Montelupo and not the finer factories. The Merida ware, with some two hundred and fifty vessels, shows a wider range of types than from any other site, while the olive jares are surprisingly few in view of their wide distribution in North-West Europe.

French imports, just over one hundred, are only half as many as from Italy, showing a marked contrast with the medieval predominance of French pottery imports. In view of the proximity of Northern France, it is interesting to see the medieval pattern of large numbers of Saintonge imports continued. Examples of Normandy stoneware, Martincamp and Beauvais wares are rare, the lack of Beauvais being due to the late date, as its peak was in the 16th century.

Netherlands wares account for the second largest group of imports, with a remarkable quantity of tin-glazed wares of the 17th century, approximately five hundred, while British tin-glaze is surprisingly rare, the position only being reversed by the 18th century. There are almost two hundred examples of Dutch lead-glazed wares, almost half being decorated slipwares, with the other half either plain brown-glazed or slipped overall in one colour.

The German wares represent almost four hundred vessels in all, but as their dates spread over the 16th to 18th centuries, the number for any one time is not nearly so large as the total might suggest. As may be expected from a deposit with little material earlier than 1550, the Raeren, Langerwehe and Siegburg wares account for only some thirty vessels. The main bulk of some two hundred vessels comprises slip and stonewares of the later 16th and 17th centuries with some tin-glazed wares. There are almost one hundred late 17th- and 18th-century Westerwald stoneware vessels. After the rise of the British pottery industries in the second half of the 17th century, this was almost the only pottery imported in addition to Chinese porcelain.

The results of the quantification therefore, give a tantalising glimpse of 16th- and 17th-century trade patterns as evidenced by the pottery. It is hoped that when other major groups are published, such as those from Poole, London, Norwich and Hull, a more precise picture will emerge, but the stratified finds are usually small in quantity, with the major examples unstratified. Recent work in Chester (Davey and Rutter, 1977) is of interest in extending the distribution of import types, but the quantities are hardly significant enough to make firm deductions. Plymouth, therefore, provides the best evidence (despite its imperfections) for proportions of various imports.

THE CATALOGUE

BRITAIN

COARSE WARES (Figs 1–18)

The term 'coarse wares' refers to that class of pottery made from the most common clays, usually red earthenwares, as is the case with the Devon and Somerset potteries, but sometimes paler earthenwares, for example, those clays from Hampshire. This term also implies a comparison with 'fine' or 'exotic' wares from far away places with greater expertise and finesse inherent in their pottery traditions.

As is the case with all study, one answer raises many questions. It would be convenient if all kitchen articles were found to be made of coarse ware, and all the table ware of fine pottery. However, this is not so: chafing dishes, for example, are well represented in both categories, and are also known to have been made of metal. Again, it would be convenient for classification purposes if the products from each area reflected the local produce, such as wine bottles from South West France, cider jars from Somerset, or fish pots from North Devon. But there is hardly a suspicion of this, and the fine wares include several forms that are present in the coarse wares. Why should this be? Does the pottery represent direct or indirect trade? Was it traded in its own right? Or did it arrive as a secondary trade dependent on the large bulk merchandise such as wool or metals?

Obviously it would be unwise to consider each class of pottery independently as one is influenced by the other, as well as by many other factors which cannot be included in a statistical analysis, for we do not know the proportion of wood, metal, bone, horn, leather or basketry articles in contemporary use with this pottery. Many of these materials could be re-used, unlike the pottery, and again unlike the pottery, many of these materials rot or corrode when thrown away or buried. However, what we do know about the individual items is stated, and what we do not know is implied by omission.

Archaeology is about people, and this pottery catalogue must stimulate certain questions about the people who made, and used this pottery. What did they eat and drink from it? How did they cook their food? How did it differ from our own? How were these foods, drinks, and wares brought to the Plymouth market? By pack horse, or boat? Many of these questions are too complicated and far reaching to contemplate answering here. Nevertheless, if the element of wonder is removed from the study of these artifacts, knowledge will not advance as quickly, and our search for the true answers in these matters will be less stimulating. The reader who is particularly interested in these general questions is recommended to look at *English Bread and Yeast Cookery*, E David, 1977; *The World We Have Lost*, P Laslett, 1971; *The English Medieval Feast*, W E Mead, 1967; *Cooking and Eating*, K Stewart, 1975; *Studies in Elizabethan Foreign Trade*, T S Willan, 1959. Specific sources of information are referred to in the body of the catalogue.

A selection only of the most complete examples of each type of pottery has been described and illustrated. The total number of sherds and the minimum number of vessels of each type is listed at the end of this catalogue section. The proportion of one type to another and an indication of the total amount of pottery from the site is to be found in the chapter on quantification (p 2)

DONYATT POTTERY, SOMERSET

Donyatt is situated between Taunton and Chard, and is near Ilminster, Somerset. According to current knowledge it started production in the early medieval period, but its height of production was between 1600 and 1800. Its products have been recognised at Taunton (Ralegh-Radford and Hallam, 1953, pp 81–8) and Exeter (Greenfield 1964, pp 357–73) but easily the best dating evidence is to be found in Bristol (Barton, 1964). For material found during actual excavations at the pottery sites at Donyatt, see Coleman-Smith and Pearson (1970) and Coleman-Smith, Pearson with Morley and others (forthcoming). (See also Noël-Hume 1976, p 107, fig 29.)

The examples of Donyatt pottery from Plymouth which are to be published in *The Donyatt Potteries, Somerset* (Coleman-Smith and Pearson, forthcoming) are not illustrated here. They are listed below with the catalogue numbers to be used in that publication.

Cups and porringers: 7/48, 7/49, 7/68, and 7/69, all of 18th century date

Dishes: 8/49, 8/53, 8/56, 8/58, 8/59, 8/60, 8/61, 8/62, 8/67, 8/90, date range 1600–50; and 8/104 and 8/152, dated to the last half of the 18th century

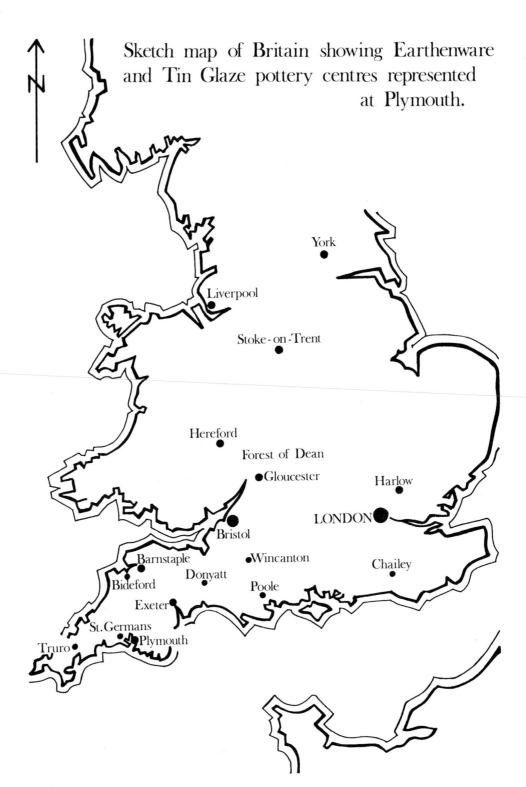

Sketch map of Britain showing Earthenware and Tin Glaze pottery centres represented at Plymouth.

York

Liverpool

Stoke - on -Trent

Hereford

Forest of Dean

Gloucester

Harlow

LONDON

Bristol

Barnstaple

Wincanton

Chailey

Donyatt

Bideford

Poole

Exeter

St. Germans

Truro

Plymouth

MAP 2

Chafing dishes: 9/12, dated to between 1600–50, and 9/38, of 18th century date

Bucket pots: 11/13, date 1600–50

Jars: 14/14, 14/49, 14/53, covering a date range 1650–1750

Chamber pots: 27/1 date 1600–50

Black manganese glazed Donyatt wares were noted at Plymouth, including cups, pedestal cups, jugs and mugs, but were very fragmentary.

The dating evidence for the Donyatt pottery will be found in full in Coleman-Smith and Pearson (forthcoming), in Barton (1964) and Ralegh-Radford and Hallam (1953). The recent and forthcoming publications of the Committee for Rescue Archaeology in Avon, Gloucestershire and Somerset do much to corroborate these dating criteria.

1 Bowl rim, pink buff fabric, coated internally with white slip with combed decoration, under a thin internal amber glaze. The decorative motif is well paralleled in Coleman-Smith and Pearson (forthcoming) 8/88, 8/89, 8/90 and others.
1600–1650.

2 Shoulder sherd, probably from a bottle, pink buff fabric with a band of white slip with combed decoration, under a thin amber glaze. For parallels see Coleman-Smith and Pearson (forthcoming) 4/226, 4/227 and 4/231.
1600–1650.

3 Plate rim, light buff red fabric, decorated internally with white slip painting under an internal amber to green, slightly reduced glaze. For a parallel see Coleman-Smith and Pearson (forthcoming) 8/94.
1600–1650.

4 Plate rim, light buff red fabric, decorated internally with bands of white slip and combed decoration, under a thin internal amber glaze. For a parallel see Coleman-Smith and Pearson (forthcoming) 8/89.
1600–1650.

5 Dish, sandy pink buff fabric, internal white slip with sgraffito decoration of tulips, under a dirty amber glaze flecked with copper. No exact parallel for this dish is to be found in the Donyatt Catalogue, however the cross-section is very similar to Coleman-Smith and Pearson (forthcoming) 8/28, which is dated *1680*, and certainly the decoration is similar to that of the *1650–1750* style, see 8/44.

6 Plate, light buff red fabric, with wide internal bands of white slip, decorated with combed decoration under an internal light amber glaze. Knife trimmed externally. For a parallel see Coleman-Smith and Pearson (forthcoming) 8/67.
1650–1750.

7 Dish, sandy pink buff fabric, internal white slip coating with sgraffito decoration under a copper green flecked amber glaze. An almost exact parallel is to be found in Coleman-Smith and Pearson (forthcoming) 8/135.
1700–1750.

8 Dish, with pie crust rim decoration, pink buff fabric, internal white slip with sgraffito decoration under a pale amber glaze with some copper flecking. Very close parallels for this decoration and pie crust rim are to be found in Coleman-Smith and Pearson (forthcoming) 8/139 and 8/140. This dish was almost certainly made at Donyatt Site 4.
1700–1750.

9 Dish base, with rim missing, pink buff fabric with internal white slip, sgraffito decorated under a pale amber glaze with some copper green flecking.
Probably 1700–1750.

10 Porringer, light buff red fabric of Donyatt pottery, decorated internally with white slip splashing under an amber glaze. For a parallel see Coleman-Smith and Pearson (forthcoming) 7/82.
1700–1750.

11 Jar rim, light buff red fabric, decorated on the shoulder with white slip and wet sgraffito, glazed internally with an amber glaze which has flaked badly. For a parallel see Coleman-Smith and Pearson (forthcoming) 14/45.
1700–1750.

12 Small dish, light buff red fabric, covered internally with a white slip under an internal amber glaze flecked with copper green, splashed externally. For a parallel see Coleman-Smith and Pearson (forthcoming) 8/112.
1750.

FOREST OF DEAN POTTERY

Forest of Dean pottery has been found associated with kilns in the Newent area some nine miles north-west of Gloucester, which must have been its main outlet. See Rhodes and Coleman-Smith (forthcoming); also Morgan 1956, pp 133–9.

13 Mug rim and handle, hard dark red to purple fine-grained earthenware, with an all-over metallic oily black glaze, over two turned lines.
17th century

HAMPSHIRE, WILTSHIRE, DORSET POTTERY

Very little work has been solely directed to study this group of pottery, possibly because it is usually undecorated and of a coarse nature. However, a useful account of the last pottery to work at Verwood is given in Kendrick (1959, 127–31), and a quantity of this pottery was excavated at Southampton (Platt and Coleman-Smith, 1975, vol 2, p 109–23). It has also come to light at Wincanton, Wilton, Dorchester, and Salisbury, where good examples can be seen in the museum. A light amber to rich brown manganese glaze was also used, good examples of which are on display in Salisbury Museum.

Note: It must be mentioned that represented in this group is a considerable quantity of light buff to white ware, of a fragmentary nature possibly from Poole *or* South West France. The fabric varies from a light buff to white sandy fabric, sometimes with a pink tinge. The glaze is pale yellow amber to pale orange amber, but a pale amber green to rich copper green glaze is also evident. The copper green glaze is often mottled in typical South West French tradition. Some of the handles are also of South West French type. Until the Poole kiln sites in Dorset have been investigated it will be hard to determine the full significance of this mixed group. Quantities are included either under 'Hampshire' or 'Miscellaneous Medieval.'

14   Pot with rod handle, sandy pink buff fabric, with an internal amber glaze flecked with iron brown, splashed externally.
18th–19th century

15   Dish, pink buff fabric with some small iron inclusions, internal amber glaze.
18th–19th century

16   Dish, buff pink fabric with some flint inclusions, internal amber glaze over wavy line.
18th–19th century

17   Doubled-handled meat dish, pink buff fabric, slab-built rectangular dish with vigorously pulled strap handle and handle scar, base knife trimmed, internal pale yellow amber glaze with some iron flecking. A good example of this form is found in Barton (1964, 208–9).
18th–19th century

18   Handle from a similar dish to (17) above, pink buff fabric, slab-built dish with pulled strap handle, with a large air bubble in it, knife trimmed base, internal pale yellow amber green glaze, oxidised and reduced.
18th–19th century

19   Dish with thrown handle, pink buff fabric, painted internally with white slip, thin internal amber glaze with copper green glaze.
18th–19th century

METROPOLITAN SLIPWARE

Pottery sites manufacturing this distinctive slipware have been excavated at Harlow, Essex, situated some seventeen miles north east of the metropolis which it was supplying. The earliest record of this pottery is 1250 but it was not until the 17th century that this particular class of slipware emerged (Fisher, 1960, 360–77). Both figures 11a and 11b in Fisher (1960) illustrate rim patterns exactly similar to (20) and (23) below. Another good example of this pottery is to be seen in Barton, 1975, 88. (See also Noël-Hume, 1976, 103 and 149, figs 26 and 57.) Texts and dates were sometimes incorporated in the slip trailed decoration. A large mug of this ware in the Fitzwilliam Museum, Cambridge, is dated 1632. Useful documentary evidence is given in Newton, Bibbings and Fisher, 1960. Dated examples mostly belong to the first half of the 17th century (Cox, 1953, 875–6).

20   Dish with centre missing, bright red orange fabric decorated internally with thinly trailed and raised white slip, applied while less wet than most slip trailing, under a rich even amber glaze.
17th century

21   Dish, bright red orange fabric with grey core, decorated internally with thinly trailed and raised white slip and bearing an inscription in trailing, only the letters E A survive, under a rich even amber glaze. Knife trimmed around the base. The letters E A may well belong to an inscription such as F(EA)RE GOD EVER, as the Metropolitan potters often decorated their wares with such pious texts. (Haggar, 1950, 28 and Norman and Reader, 1906, 247).
17th century

22   Dish, bright red orange fabric, decorated internally with thinly trailed and raised white slip, under a rich even amber glaze.
17th century

23   Dish, rim sherd, bright red orange fabric, decorated internally with thinly trailed and raised white slip, under a rich even amber glaze.
17th century

24   Chafing dish, bright red orange fabric, decorated internally on the rim, knob, and externally with thinly trailed white slip under a rich allover amber glaze. Holes have been made through the dish and base before firing, to allow a ready supply of air to aid the burning coals inside the dish. This is a rare example of a Metropolitan slipware chafing dish.
17th century

25   Handle, bright red orange fabric with dark grey core, decorated with thinly trailed white slip, under a rich allover amber glaze.
17th century

MIDLANDS PURPLE

'By the early 17th century a range of wares having a smooth brick-red fabric and a glossy blac iron-stained glaze had come into general use throughout a triangular area extending from Yorkshire in the north to Herefordshire in the west, and to Kent in the south-east.' (Brears, 1971, 37–9) The Forest of Dean pottery could be included in this type.

26 Baking dish sherd, perhaps from a divided dish: that is, a dish with a clay partition dividing the space into half. Hard purple-red smooth fabric, decorated internally with very white slip under a pale amber glaze.
19th century

NORTH DEVON POTTERY

The potteries of North Devon, situated in the Bideford and Barnstaple area, appear to have developed a distinctly regional type around 1600, probably to service the growing sea traffic in the two ports. No actual kiln sites have yet been excavated, probably because they were situated in the town areas, but a kiln site at Instow was owned by the Fishley family (Fishley Holland, 1958). For a most useful paper on the pottery see Watkins, 1960. (See also Noël-Hume, 1976, 105–6, fig 28 and Cotter, 1958.)

27 Bowl, light buff red fabric with gravel inclusions, internal rich amber glaze.
17th century or later

28 Bowl rim, light buff red fabric with gravel inclusions, patchy rich amber glaze.
17th century or later

29 Large bowl with handle, light buff red fabric, with gravel inclusions, patchy internal rich amber glaze.
17th century or later

30 Chafing dish rim with thrown lug, light buff red fabric with some gravel inclusions, some rich amber glaze. A slightly different form of chafing dish of North Devon manufacture is to be found in Platt (1962, 222, no 17).
17th century

31 Chamber pot, with handle and base missing, light buff red fabric with rich internal amber glaze splashed externally.
17th century or later

32 Chamber pot rim, light buff red to grey fabric, decorated externally with white slip and sgraffito decoration under a rich amber glaze. This form is closely paralleled in Watkins (1960, fig 5).
17th century or later

33 Cistern base with spigot spout, light buff fabric with gravel inclusions, internal badly developed amber glaze.
17th century or later

34 Probably a cistern base, but the spigot spout is missing from this sherd. Light buff fabric with gravel inclusions, internal amber glaze.
17th century or later

35 Cup, light buff red fabric, decorated externally with white slip and sgraffito decoration of tulips and flowers under a rich amber glaze. A very close parallel is to be seen in Watkins (1960, 18, fig 1).
17th century or later

36 Straight sided dish. Light buff red fabric with gravel inclusions, internal rich amber glaze.
17th century or later

37 Jar rim with return handle, light buff red fabric with gravel inclusions, internal rich amber glaze, splashed externally.
17th century or later

38 Tall jar rim, similar in form to (39) below, but with no turned line, light buff fabric with gravel inclusions.
17th century or later

39 Tall jar of baluster shape, light buff red fabric with gravel inclusions. One turned line on shoulder, internal patchy rich amber glaze.
17th century or later

40 Jar rim with rod handle, thumbed and applied strip around rim, light buff fabric with gravel inclusions, internal amber glaze.
17th century or later

41 Jug rim with pulled lip and rod handle, light red to buff fabric with some gravel inclusions, allover rich amber glaze.
17th century or later

42 Jug neck with pulled lip, light buff red fabric with some gravel inclusions, external white slip under an allover rich amber glaze.
17th century or later

43 Perforated knob, hard red to buff grey fabric with some gravel inclusions. Perforated three times, once through centre top, twice each side of the same quarter as a semi-circular break, possibly from a watering pot, external rich amber to green glaze.
17th century or later

44 Large pan rim, probably from an elliptical salting pan, light buff red fabric with gravel inclusions, with heavy rod handle, rich internal amber glaze, splashed externally.
17th century or later

45 Large pan rim, light buff fabric with gravel inclusions, with a thumbed and applied strip under the rim, internal rich patchy amber glaze.
17th century or later

46 Pancheon, light buff red fabric with gravel inclusions, rich brown to amber glaze internally.
17th century or later

47 Pancheon, light buff fabric with some gravel inclusions, rich internal amber glaze.
17th century or later

48 Pancheon, light buff red fabric with gravel inclusions, internal rich amber glaze.
17th century or later

49 Pancheon, light buff red fabric with gravel inclusions, rich brown to amber glaze splashed externally.
17th century or later

50 Plate centre, hard light red to buff grey fabric, decorated with internal white slip and sgraffito design of part of a bird, under a rich amber glaze.
17th century or later

51 Plate, hard light red to buff fabric, decorated with internal white slip and sgraffito design of part of a bird, under a rich amber glaze, knife trimmed externally.
17th century or later

52 Plate, hard light red to buff fabric, decorated internally with white slip and sgraffito design of a floral motif, probably a tulip. Areas filled with typical comb pecking under a rich amber glaze, knife trimmed externally.
17th century or later

53 Plate sherd, light buff red fabric, decorated internally with white slip and sgraffito under a rich amber glaze.
17th century or later

54 Plate, hard light red to buff fabric, decorated internally with white slip and sgraffito design of geometric pattern under a rich amber glaze, knife trimmed externally. For a very close parallel see Watkins (1960, 32).
17th century

55 Plate sherd, light buff red fabric, decorated with white slip and sgraffito under a rich amber glaze, knife trimmed externally.
17th century or later

56 Plate sherd, light buff red fabric, decorated internally with white slip and sgraffito decoration under a rich amber glaze, knife trimmed.
17th century or later

57 Plate rim, light buff red fabric, decorated internally with white slip and sgraffito decoration, under a rich amber glaze.
17th century or later

58 Porringer with handle missing, light buff red fabric with some gravel inclusions under a rich amber glaze running unevenly externally, and with kiln scars.
17th century or later

59 Porringer with horizontal handle, light red buff fabric, with internal white slip under a rich internal amber glaze running externally; foot missing.
17th century or later

60 Rims, light buff red fabric with some gravel
64 inclusions rich amber glaze splashed externally.
17th century or later

65 Barrel costrel, light red buff fabric with gravel inclusions, with a patchy rich amber glaze externally. Barrel costrels are well represented in the south and west of England, as early as the 13th century at Laverstock (Musty, Algar and Ewence, 1969, 133, fig 22) and the 14th century (Shortt, 1960, 23). Two local costrels in the Torquay Museum are of 15th- and 17th-century dates respectively (Ralegh-Radford and Rogers, 1953, 29). At Donyatt barrel costrels were being made as early as the 14th century and continued to be part of the potters' products until as late as 1851 (Coleman-Smith and Pearson, forthcoming, 2/1 to 2/14).
17th to 19th century

66 Bottle costrel, light red buff fabric with gravel inclusions, with a patchy rich amber glaze externally.
17th to 19th century

67 Dish with thrown handle, similar in form to (19) in Hampshire pottery. Light red buff fabric with gravel inclusions, rich internal amber glaze stained copper green which is unusual for North Devon products.
18th to 19th century

68 Ladle, light red buff fabric with gravel inclusions, rich amber glaze inside bowl. The handle is pulled. Although ceramic ladles are known from Saxo-Norman times, this is the first record of a North Devon one.
18th to 19th century

Note: A procedure which is often to be noted in North Devon jugs with pulled spouts and rod handles is that the neck is made in a light buff-red fabric *with* gravel inclusions, while the handle is pulled in a slightly redder fabric with no gravel inclusions.

SOUTH WEST MICACEOUS (ST GERMANS TYPE) POTTERY

St Germans is situated some six miles west of Plymouth, and is in the county of Cornwall. It is sited on a tributary of the Tamar River, namely the St Germans or Lynher River. A kiln site was excavated there by E Greenfield following trial digging by Mrs M Minter and Miss V Russell (Medieval Archaeol 1, 1957, 170). The kiln site is to be published shortly by K. Barton. The provisional date for the kiln is 1450–1550 but it is obvious from the assemblage at Plymouth that potters using a similar clay source were producing pottery well after this date, probably into the 17th century. Stray finds of micaceous wares have come from Cardinham, Cornwall, and Ivybridge, Kingsbridge and South Brent, Devon (Plymouth Museum) and occur amongst the material from the Tintagel excavations (Truro Museum). It is clear that clays derived from the granite masses of the southwest peninsula were widely used; only further detailed study will enable this large group of pottery to be better defined.

69 Base with thumbed foot rim, dark grey buff fabric with grey core, flecked with quartz

and mica. The applied foot rim is thumbed neatly underneath, and was obviously meant to stabilise the sagging base. Unglazed.
15th century or later

70 Base with thumbed foot rim, buff red fabric with grey core, flecked with quartz and mica. The applied foot rim has been thumbed neatly underneath and has been square jabbed at regular 2 mm distances at the inside join with the body. Unglazed.
15th century or later

71 Two body sherds, light grey to red fabric, flecked with quartz and mica with dark grey core, painted externally with thin white slip painting.
15th century or later

72 Body sherd, 13 cm radius, dark grey fabric with buff interior, flecked with quartz and mica, painted externally with white slip.
15th century or later

73 Body sherd with strap handle base, grey buff fabric flecked with quartz and mica, painted externally with white slip. The handle is knife jabbed.
15th century or later

74 Body sherd with strap handle base, grey buff fabric flecked with quartz and mica. The handle is jabbed.
15th century or later

75 Bowl rim, dark grey buff fabric flecked with quartz and mica, decorated externally with white slip painting, glazed internally with a rich amber glaze.
15th century or later

76 Bowl rim, dark grey buff fabric, flecked with quartz and mica, decorated externally with thin white slip painting, glazed internally with a patchy green amber glaze.
15th century or later

77 Possibly a chafing dish base, buff red fabric with grey core, flecked with quartz and mica. Comb decoration and square jabbing.
15th century or later

78 Candlestick base with rod handle, grey buff to red fabric with thin grey core, flecked with quartz and mica.
15th century or later

79 Cistern base with spigot spout, dark grey fabric flecked with quartz and mica.
15th century or later

80 Cresset lamp, dark grey to red fabric with grey core, flecked with quartz and mica. Unglazed.
15th century or later

81 Cooking pot, grey buff to red fabric flecked with quartz and mica, painted externally with white slip painting.
15th century or later

82 Cooking pot return handle, similar to the Dutch contemporaries, buff red fabric with thin grey core, flecked with quartz and mica.

The handle is knife slashed at the elbow, and once at the junction with the body. Unglazed.
15th century or later

83 Dish, buff red fabric with quartz and mica flecking, knife trimmed externally. The internal glaze is much overfired and is bubbled and discoloured, possibly in refuse fires.
15th century or later

84 Frying pan handle, hard grey buff fabric flecked with quartz and mica, glazed towards the inside base with a rich amber glaze.
15th century or later

85 Strap handle, grey fabric flecked with quartz and mica. The handle is jabbed.
15th century or later

86 Jar neck, dark grey buff fabric, flecked with quartz and mica, decorated externally with thin white slip painting. Unglazed.
15th century or later

87 Jar neck, dark grey buff fabric, flecked with quartz and mica, decorated externally with thin white slip painting which has run slightly. Unglazed.
15th century or later

88 Neck and shoulder of large vessel, dark grey buff fabric flecked with quartz and mica, with grey core. Decorated externally with thin white slip painting.
15th century or later

89 Pancheon rim, dark grey buff fabric, flecked with quartz and mica, with grey core, decorated internally with a white slip painted band.
15th century or later

90 Pancheon with wide pulled lip, base missing, dark grey buff red fabric flecked with quartz and mica, with grey core, decorated internally with a white slip painted band, glazed internally on the lower half only, with a rich amber glaze.
15th century or later

91 Large vessel with sagging base, buff red fabric with pale grey core, flecked with quartz and mica.
15th century or later

92 Pan sherd, buff to grey fabric, flecked with quartz and mica, burned red externally, possibly through use. Internal amber glaze.
15th century or later

STAFFORDSHIRE/BRISTOL SLIPWARE

This class of pottery is made from the 'can clays' that are found associated with coal seams. It has a light buff yellow fabric when oxidised. Its actual manufacture is described in Plot (1686). See also Rackham (1951) who illustrates most of the classes of pottery illustrated here. However, a very similar slipware was also produced at Bristol. The evidence for this is to be found in Barton

(1964). (See also Noël-Hume, 1976, 107 and 136, figs 29 and 51.)

93   Base, of light yellow buff fabric decorated externally with a rich dark brown to black slip, trailed with a white slip and feathered, under a thin even amber glaze much stained by the slip. Similar to Celoria and Kelly (1973, 64, no 88).
18th century

94   Bowl, of light yellow buff fabric, decorated internally with wide rich dark brown to black slip trailing under a thin even amber glaze.
18th century

95   Cup with handle missing, of light yellow buff fabric, decorated externally with rich dark brown to black slip dots and feathering. Iron from the slip has stained the thin amber glaze. Similar to Celoria and Kelly (1973, 75, no 239).
18th century

96   Porringer, with base missing, of light yellow buff fabric, decorated externally with a rich dark brown to black slip dotted onto the rim and banded onto the body which has then been further embellished with white slip trailing under a thin even amber glaze, stained by the brown slip.
18th century

97   Dish pressed over a mould, light yellow buff fabric, decorated internally with dark brown to black slip feathering under a thin even amber glaze. The rim is impressed on the edge to give a pie crust effect. For close parallels see Celoria and Kelly (1973, 86–7) and Rackham (1951, fig 1).
Late 17th or early 18th century

98   Dish pressed over a mould, light yellow buff fabric decorated internally with a rich dark brown to black slip and wide white slip trailing, under a thin amber glaze. The rim is impressed on the edge. See Celoria and Kelly (1973, 86–7).
18th century

99   Dish, pressed over a mould, light yellow buff fabric decorated internally with a rich dark brown to black feathering under a thin even amber glaze. The rim is impressed on the edge. See Celoria and Kelly (1973, 77).
18th century

100   Rim, of light yellow buff fabric, decorated externally by rich dark brown to black slip trailing under a thin even amber glaze.
18th century

101   Rim, of light yellow buff fabric, decorated externally with a rich dark brown to black slip trailing, under a thin even amber glaze.
18th century

STAFFORDSHIRE REDWARE AND AGATE WARE

These are well-known as Staffordshire wares, 1720–50. They have hard fine-grained fabrics of red earthenware, known in the potteries as 'tea pot clay', usually glazed with a transparent, thin, even glaze which enhances the fabric colour to a rich chestnut red. Examples are often marbled with a dark brown slip, and fine turned thin profiles are typical. It would be interesting to know from what geological strata this clay was obtained. Both the Redware and the Agate Ware fabrics are similar in body and glaze to excavated sherds from the pot works at Pamona Inn, Newcastle-under-Lyme, Staffs. (Information from J Kelly, City Museum and Art Gallery, Stoke-on-Trent.) (See also Bemrose, 1973.) Not illustrated, as sherds are too fragmentary. *Date range 1720–1750.*

SUSSEX POTTERY

One of the best known centres of production was at Chailey, some ten miles north-east of Brighton, but many other potteries existed in this county (Mainwaring Baines, 1948, and Dawson, 1903, 28–32).

102   Bowl, hard red fabric with some iron inclusions, internal rich amber brown glaze flecked with iron. Sussex, probably Chailey.
18th century

MISCELLANEOUS MEDIEVAL

103   Spout, possibly from a spouted pitcher, smooth grey buff fabric with grey external coating. Unglazed.
Possibly medieval.

BRITAIN: QUANTITIES

DONYATT POTTERY QUANTITIES

Form		Sherds	Min Vessels	
1500–1600				
Cup (lobed)		1	1	small sherds very weathered
Cistern		12	8	and eroded
	TOTAL	13	9	
1600–1650				
Decorated Jar		15	10	external sgraffito decoration
Bowl		5	3	
Bottle		3	2	
Plate		8	6	
	TOTAL	31	21	
circa 1650				
Cup/Mug (brown glaze)		210	46	some examples with encrusted quartz in slip decoration
Jug (brown glaze)		145	38	some examples with incised line decoration
Misc. (brown glaze)		85	—	small cup/jug sherds
	TOTAL	440	84	
1650–1700				
Dish		3,701	1,485	sgraffito, slip-trailed and plain forms
Bowl		1,238	635	plain, medium size
Bowl		233	88	slip-trailed and sgraffito
Small Bowl		81	68	shallow, internal brown-green glaze
Large Bowl		70	33	
Bowl/Jar		400	—	
Bowl/Jar/Jug		1,061	185	small vessels, body and base sherds
Bowl/Jar/Pancheon		201	—	large vessels, body sherds only
Jar		33	28	large jars; rim sherds
Large jar/Crock		7	7	rim sherds
Pancheon		216	93	rim and base sherds
Large Crock		12	12	
Jug		134	104	
Porringer		1,052	296	minimum based on rim sherds
Ladle		5	5	5 lug handles; 2 types—flush with rim and below rim
Chamber Pot		132	65	
Colander		6	4	square 'nail' holes pierced in base
Chafing Dish		68	20	2 types—(6 sh) with upright lugs; (1 sh) with cut-out areas in rim. See Coleman-Smith and Pearson, forthcoming
Pipkin		58	38	(29 feet) rod and strap handles, wiped white slip on shoulder and banded white slip with wavy line through
Baking Dish		22	11	6 lug handles
Shallow Pan		12	3	2 rims with pulled spout
Bottle Costrel		4	3	lug handles
Miscellaneous		55	—	
	TOTAL	8,801	3,183	

(continued)

1700–1750

Dish	77	46	sgraffito decoration
Bucket Pot	13	6	slip-trailed decoration on shoulder. See Coleman-Smith and Pearson, 1970 fig 4 nos 1 and 2
Chamber Pot	6	5	external slip-trailed decoration on shoulder and rim
Porringer	27	16	spattered slip and trailed decoration
Jar	53	38	
Small Dish	3	3	
TOTAL	179	114	
DONYATT TOTALS	9,464	3,411	

FOREST OF DEAN POTTERY QUANTITIES

1600–1700

Form	Sherds	Min Vessels
Mug	7	6
TOTAL	7	6

HAMPSHIRE, WILTSHIRE, DORSET POTTERY QUANTITIES

Form	Sherds	Min Vessels	

1600–1700   Hants/Wilts manganese-glazed wares

Puzzle Jug	1	1	neck sherds with circular holes pierced through. See examples in Salisbury Museum.
Chafing Dish	1	1	with upright mushroom lug
Large Dish	5	3	
Shallow Dish/Plate	5	2	
Bowl	9	8	
Jug	5	3	
Cup/Mug	29	18	plain with allover glaze
Cup/Mug	4	4	with incised combed decoration under allover glaze
TOTAL	59	40	

1700–1900   White painted fabric with orange-green-yellow lead glazes

Jar	715	182	
Small Bowl/Porringer	203	78	
Chafing Dish	16	14	
Jug	37	34	
Pipkin	17	14	
Cistern	1	1	
Jug/Jar	391	—	body sherds
Mug/Cup/Porringer	426	198	
Mug/Cup/Porringer	18	18	handles
Baking Dish	116	45	
Large Jar	44	18	
Pancheon	24	19	
Chamber Pot	6	6	
Dish	22	18	
Ointment Pot	12	12	
Miscellaneous	666	—	
TOTAL	2,714	657	

1700–1800 Very chalky white fabric, smoother than above group, with blocky fractures. None illustrated.

Small bowl	3	2	internally and externally green lead glazed
Jug	10	3	internal and external orange brown lead glaze
Candlestick	3	2	glazed as jug above
Press moulded dish	11	4	internally red slipped, white slip-trailed and feathered. Similar and probably imitating Staffordshire/Bristol yellow slipware.
Tankard	1	1	internal and external patchy yellow glaze
Jar	1	1	external patchy yellow glaze; slightly pink fabric of the same texture as above
Small Cup/Mug	11	10	yellow to orange glaze
Bowl/Posset Cup	1	1	external yellow glaze
TOTAL	41	24	

LOCAL RED EARTHENWARE QUANTITIES

Form	Sherds	Min Vessels
1850–1930?		
Pancheon	76	13
Chimney Pot	28	6
Miscellaneous	138	—
	242	19

LATE 19th CENTURY STONEWARE QUANTITIES

128 sherds   Miscellaneous forms

METROPOLITAN SLIPWARE QUANTITIES

Form	Sherds	Min Vessels	
1600–1700			
Small Dish	14	11	slip-trailed designs
Chafing Dish	2	1	
Dish	6	5	
Handle	1	1	
Miscellaneous	2	2	
TOTAL	25	20	

MIDLANDS PURPLE QUANTITIES

Form	Sherds	Min Vessels	
1600–1900			
Dish, press-moulded	85	68	Slip-trailed, some highly decorated. Included in this type because the fabric is a brick-red to purple colour often with striations of white clay. They are similar to Staffs/Bristol press-moulded dishes, and these hard red purple clays can be found in both areas. None illustrated.
Porringer/Bowl	65	18	
Bowl	239	45	
Pancheon	64	38	
Porringer	37	21	
Mug	10	6	
Plate	1	1	
Lid	1	1	
Dish	33	30	
Baking Dish	1	1	probably divided
Cup	4	4	
TOTAL	542	233	

NORTH DEVON POTTERY QUANTITIES

Form	Sherds	Min Vessels	
1600–1700 or later			
Dish	150	57	plain undecorated forms
	515	190	decorated forms, sgraffito floral, asymmetrical and symmetrical patterns; rim diameters from 26 cm to 36 cm.
Bowl	137	98	rims
Large Jar	136	62	
Pilchard Jar	820	343	rim and base sherds
Jar	741	236	
Jar/Jug/Bowl	15,600	—	body sherds, unquantifiable
Pancheon	486	173	
Pan	9	6	
Salting Pan	19	10	oval form
Jug	415	98	plain with pulled spout; min no of vessels based on rim sherds.
Cistern	23	23	based on bung holes
Porringer	103	76	plain undecorated forms with internal white slip; horizontal and vertical handles.
	1	1	sgraffito decoration; horizontal and vertical handles.
Mug	3	3	
Cup/Small Jug	6	—	
Large Cresset Lamp	8	7	
Cresset Lamp	1	1	
Spittoon	1	1	
Candlestick	1	1	
Chafing Dish	50	38	
Bottle Costrel	2	2	lug handles
Barrel Costrel	6	4	
Baking Dish	19	13	1 example divided
Pipkin	38	13	24 feet (tripod form)
Ladle	1	1	
Chamber Pot	38	17	plain rims with external sgraffito decoration
	112	102	rim sherds; 30 handles
Watering Can	3	2	
Pedestal Base	2	2	
Decorated Jar	1	1	external sgraffito decoration
Cup	15	8	
Straight-sided Dish	13	9	
Plate	63	48	
Miscellaneous	5	—	
TOTAL	19,543	1,646	

STAFFORDSHIRE/BRISTOL MANGANESE GLAZED WARE QUANTITIES

Form	Sherds	Min Vessels	
1680–1750			
Mug/Tankard	119	43	Not illustrated

STAFFORDSHIRE RED WARE QUANTITIES

1700–1750			
Bowl	2	2	Not illustrated

STAFFORDSHIRE AGATE WARE QUANTITIES

1700–1750			
Knob	1	1	Not illustrated

SOUTH WEST MICACEOUS QUANTITIES

Form	Sherds	Min Vessels	
1400–1500 or later	Some sherds in this group may have been partly wasted during firing and sold as 'seconds'.		
Pipkin	18	17	
Chafing Dish	2	2	
Platter	2	2	
Candlestick	2	2	
Cresset Lamp	2	2	
Jar	22	20	
Pancheon	202	176	1 base sherd with a piece of slate glazed on its bottom, possibly a kiln 'placer'.
Bowl	240	158	One handled
Roasting Tray	5	4	
Large Jar	80	56	
Cistern	74	67	
Ridge Tile	45	31	
Chimney Pot	2	2	
Jug/Jar	289	—	unidentifiable body sherds
Miscellaneous	8,526	—	body sherds from bowl/jar/jug/cistern forms
TOTAL	9,767	774	

Medieval Type Sherds			
Spouted Pitcher	2	2	
Jug/Cistern	13	12	
Miscellaneous sherds	75	—	
TOTAL	90	14	

SUSSEX POTTERY QUANTITIES

Form	Sherds	Min Vessels
1700–1800		
Pancheon	24	13
Pan	3	3
Jar	42	27
Bowl	2	2
Miscellaneous	33	—
TOTAL	104	45

MISCELLANEOUS MEDIEVAL QUANTITIES

342 sherds This group includes 287 body sherds of English/French white fabric.

MISCELLANEOUS POST MEDIEVAL QUANTITIES

643 sherds Various forms, body sherds.

CHINA

PORCELAIN

For convenience this large group of porcelain has been divided by style into the main centuries to which it belongs. There have been problems of specific identification, in many cases due to the deterioration of the enamels, so that the precise colour is often obscured. Broadly speaking, the forms fall into three main categories: cups, bowls (small and large) and plates. The cups are handleless. The large bowls are generally characterised by their large footrings.

17th (AND POSSIBLY 16th) CENTURY

I. 'Carrack' porcelain (so-called because it was transported in Portugese carracks), made in the Ming dynasty under the Emperor Wan-Li, dates c1590–1620. This group is characterised by underglaze blue outline-and-wash designs. The plates often have central designs of flowers, deer (which in Chinese mythology are associated with the god of long life) or auspicious emblems such as a tied-up scroll representing literature.

Cups/Bowls
4 rims; 7 bases of fluted bowls.

Plates
3 rims; 15 bases: 12 sherds.

II. 'Transitional' period wares. Vessels in this group probably belong to the first half of the century (although the 'transition period' extends beyond 1650) and have mostly abstract floral or geometric designs in underglaze blue. Several bases of plates have grits on the underside.

Bowls
7 large bowl bases; 6 small bowl bases.

Plates
11 sherds (1 with long life symbol in Chinese characters).

III. Provincial wares. These were not manufactured at the main centres, and although they are painted in underglaze blue they are quite distinctive as the glaze and general quality is not so fine.

Bowls
1 rim; 3 bases.

IV. Not a very distinctive group but the vessels are painted in underglaze blue and seem to fall within the date range 1650–80.

Bowls/Cups
7 rims; 8 bases; 14 sherds.

V. Rim of a small cup which is green all over, c1690–1700.

Cups
1 rim.

VI. 'Famille verte' with red and strong bright green enamels. This ware was made under the Emperor K'ang Hsi, and dates to the late 17th or early 18th centuries.

Bowls
2 sherds.

VII. Late 17th to early 18th century. One cup with an everted rim and underglaze grey-blue external decoration. One fragment of a stem cup.

Cups
1 cup; 1 fragment.

18th CENTURY

I. Blue and white porcelain with dragon decoration. The dragon is 'bearded' and flies through blue clouds. First half of the century.

Bowls
23 rims; 5 bases.

Plates
4 bases; 48 sherds.

II. Porcelains with 'cafe au lait' generally brown glaze covering the exterior. All this group are cups and date to 1710–35.

Brown Glaze Cups
7 rims without enamels; 7 bases without enamels; 3 sherds without enamels; 1 rim with enamel; 1 base with enamel.

Blue Glaze Cups
1 rim; 1 base (possibly from one vessel).

III. 'Chinese Imari' style wares with underglaze blue and gold and red enamel decoration. All have abstract or floral decoration with the exception of one large bowl which has a landscape scene. c1710–35.

Cups
12 rims; 9 bases.

Bowls
33 rims of large bowls; 3 bases of large bowls; 2 bases of small bowls; 2 rims of fluted bowls.

Plates/Dishes
7 bases; 1 small shallow dish.

IV. Porcelains decorated in enamels (the exact colour is often no longer clear). This group has predominantly bright orange-red and gold spiky scroll decoration interspersed with flowers, and generally surrounding flowers with foliage and either pink or yellow petals. If the original enamels were those of the 'famille verte', a date c1700–25 could be assigned; if the rose-pink of the 'famille rose' appears, a somewhat later date would apply. Two sherds depict a gold and red-orange grasshopper (?).

Bowls
6 rims, including 1 hexagonal; 1 base from large bowl; 8 sherds.

V. Small bowl with bright orange-red and green enamel decoration on the exterior, partly depicting a water plant. The central motif at the base of the interior is a rather poorly executed underglaze blue design *c*1720–40.

VI. Typical blue and white flower plate with a geometric and floral border. 1730–40.

VII. Large group of blue and white porcelain which can be broadly dated to the second half of the century. The rims often have 'ferronerie' type diaper or honeycomb border patterns which were designed for export. The exteriors are usually decorated with landscape scenes and include figures crossing bridges.

Bowls
66 rims; 3 large bases; 63 small bases.

Plates
5 rims; 16 bases; 170 miscellaneous rims; 526 sherds.

VIIIa. 'Famille rose' and related enamels, *c*1730–80. These have underglaze blue decoration with red-orange, green, pink, yellow and gold enamels.

Cups
3 rims.

Bowls
17 large rims; 7 bases; 5 small rims; 6 shallow bowl rims; 12 bowls/dishes bases; 3 hexagonal bowl rims.

Cylindrical Jar with lid seating
1 rim.

Mugs
1 base.

Plates
1 rim; 1 base; 20 sherds with exterior decoration; 4 sherds with interior decoration.

VIIIb. 'Famille rose' and related enamels, *c*1730–80. Mainly flower and figure designs.

Bowls/Cups
36 rims; 16 bases with exterior decoration; 4 large bowl bases; 32 sherds with exterior decoration.

Plates
58 bases, 3 of them fluted.

IXa. Swatow stoneware in a red fabric with bright orange-red and green abstract floral decoration.

Bowls, Large
9 sherds.

Bowls
1 rim.

IXb. Blue and white Swatow.

Bowls
1 rim; 3 sherds.

Plates
2 rims; 3 bases.

IXc. Late 18th century Swatow.

Bowls
1 rim.

Plates
1 large portion.

FAR EAST

MARTABANI (Fig 19)

Martabani jars, thought to have originated in Java *c*200 AD, were first traded by the Arabs from the port of Martaban, Burma in the 14th century. They were used for transporting crystallised fruit. In 1600 the Dutch took over the Portuguese trade. There was no direct market for them in Europe, but they were traded in Indonesia and the Philippines, where they are still used today as storage jars and water butts (Miedema, 1974).

Jars
1 rim.

104   Rim sherd from jar. Purple grey stoneware, glazed all over with dull brown temmoku glaze.

FRANCE

BEAUVAIS SGRAFFITO (Fig 19)

Single and double slip sgraffito decoration seems to have been the most widespread type produced in the 16th century at Beauvais, which lies 62 km north of Paris. A kiln at Le Detroit, dating to the first half of the 16th century, has been discovered, while finds from L'Heraule show that production continued into the late 16th and early 17th centuries. (Chami 1963, Fay 1973).

Fabric: Single Slip Sgraffito. Fine white fabric, with numerous minute red inclusions, covered with a red slip and a clear glaze. The sgraffito decoration cuts through the slip and shows as yellow cutting through red-brown.

Dishes
3 rims; 1 base; 5 sherds.

Fabric: Double Slip Sgraffito. Fabric as for Single Slip Sgraffito but the red slip is further covered by a white slip. The sgraffito decoration is then cut through the top white slip to show the red beneath, thus giving the impression of a red fabric. A clear glaze with splashes of green and blue covers the sgraffito decoration. Most sherds appear to have been wiped on the exterior surface.

London

Plymouth

Dieppe

Ger
NORMANDY Martincamp
Rouen Beauvais

Sketch map of Spain and France,
showing the principal Earthenware
and Lustre ware pottery centres.

SAINTONGE

Bordeaux

ARAGON

PORTUGAL CATALONIA

Manises
Lisbon Merida Valencia

ANDALUSIA
Seville

Malaga

MAP 3

Dishes
3 rims; 1 base; 9 sherds.

105　Flat base of double slip sgraffito dish with a sgraffito bird with folded wings cutting through to first red slip. Overall green glaze with splashes of blue.

106　Rim sherd of double slip sgraffito dish with overlapping sgraffito lines confined in a zone by two further horizontal sgraffito lines. Mainly clear glaze splashed with green.

Jugs/Jars
1 sherd.

107　Sherd of jug/jar with no internal glaze. External double slip sgraffito decoration cutting through to red slip. Glazed yellow with tinges of green.

MARTINCAMP SLIP (Fig 19)

17th century
Martincamp lies halfway between Dieppe and Beauvais, just to the west of Neufchâtel-en-Bray. Although this was known to be an important pottery centre in the 18th and 19th centuries, its earlier 17th century products have only recently been recognised, when in 1974 slipware wasters were discovered (Rogère undated, Hurst, 1977a).

Fabric: Fine white fabric with minute red inclusions. Rilling occurs on the back of the vessels which usually have hammer-headed rims and green and brown abstract slip decoration.

Dishes
4 rims; 1 base; 1 sherd.

108　One almost complete dish with typical arc border decoration and abstract floral decoration in the centre.

SAINTONGE (Figs 19–20)

Green and yellow 16th century
Saintonge is the name given to an area which lies along the Gironde estuary and which is encompassed by the River Charente. From several centres in this region both polychrome and plain wares were exported in the 13th century. The closure of trade routes caused some decline in the later 14th and 15th centuries. However, by the 16th and 17th centuries there was a considerable trade in Saintonge chafing dishes. Polychrome wares became popular again in the first half of the 17th century.

Fabric: Soft buff/white to pink fabric with red inclusions. When polychrome or glazed green or yellow there is a white slip beneath the glaze.

Chafing Dishes
Examples of chafing dishes from the Castle Street excavation have already been published in *Sixteenth-and-seventeenth-century*

chafing dishes from the Saintonge (Hurst, 1974). All the chafing dish sherds are, therefore, listed here according to the types established by Hurst and most are not illustrated.

Hurst Type I. Plain heads under small knobs. 5 yellow knobs with simple heads, 1 with holes through; 2 green; 3 unglazed knobs, 2 with traces of having had head attached.

Hurst Type II. Full length figures and complex heads cf Type IIa, fig 8, no 29, 30. Hurst, 1974. 2 heads, 6 figures.

109　Chafing dish long knob with very schematic full length figure. Green exterior and yellow interior glaze.

Hurst Type IV. cf fig 9, nos 42–46, Hurst, 1974.

Hurst Type V. Large rectangular and circular medallions. 4 faces on medallions, 2 of them unidentifiable; 1 half figure. Total of 7.

110　Large circular medallion with a swan moulded in the centre. Green internal and external glaze.

111　Large medallion consisting of two overlapping rosettes, each with a different design, the smaller one at the top. Green glazed.

112　Rectangular medallion, green glazed all over but speckled on the interior. Two animal (?) faces divided by a leaf motif on a central stem.

Hurst Type VI. Rounded knobs. Total of 8, 1 with handle.

113　Rounded knob with light green glaze on the interior, unglazed buff exterior. Thin handle projecting from beneath knob.

Hurst Type VII. Decorated handles. 3 with stab decoration; 3 with holes for applied decoration; 1 with beard (?) at top (or bottom?) of medallion.

Hurst Type VIII. Arcaded knobs. cf fig 9, no 51, 52, Hurst, 1974. Total of 56, including 4 chafing dish middles; 14 chafing dish bases; 13 plain handles.

Miscellaneous—6 unidentifiable chafing dish knobs; 4 chafing dish sherds.

114　A knob consisting of a protusion with an external finger identation in the middle. Green glazed all over.

115　Lid of half covered bowl, green glazed all over with leaf design on upper surface.

116　Unusual bowl in typical pink-buff fabric. Concave rim, possibly for lid seating. Green glazed on interior, unglazed exterior.

Note:　Because of the nature of chafing dishes with their indeterminate number of knobs and the fragmentary condition of this group, it is impossible to estimate the minimum number of vessels.

SAINTONGE LATE POLYCHROME

First half of 17th century

Fabric: Soft buff/white to pink fabric with red inclusions, a white slip beneath the glaze.

Hurst Type A II. Polychrome glazed jugs. 1 pedestal base and applied strip decoration, published, fig 2, no 5, Hurst, 1974; 1 double spouted jug, published *ibid* fig 2 no 8.

117 Sherd from jug/jar with a bright green glazed interior and an external polychrome medallion in brown, yellow and blue-green with foliage surrounding it.

Hurst Type B. Dishes and bowls. 11 rims, 6 of them upright, 2 flanged, 1 beaded; 4 bases; 5 sherds, 2 with polychrome outside but green glazed inside.

(*a*) Vessels with wide flanged scalloped rims with applied decoration. A total of 4, one already published fig 3, no 5, Hurst, 1974.

(*b*) Bowls with decorated lugs.
3 rims, one already published *ibid* fig 3, no 6; 6 lugs

(*c*) Bowls with either upright plain or everted rims and decorated with alternating coloured stripes.

118 Plain rimmed bowl with an internal creamy yellow glaze and broad short brown (one is yellow) stripes at the rim.

119 Similar to no 118 (above) but with one blue-green stripe.

120 Dish with sharply everted rim with green and brown stripes. The bottom half of the exterior is burnished.

121 Bowl with bead rim and green glazed exterior. The interior is brown with green stripes at the rim.

122 Unusual moulded rim of bowl with polychrome glaze.

Hurst Type C II. Chafing dishes.

123 Knob of usual type with roundel at the top (and presumably at the bottom) in pale creamy-green glaze outlined in a dark blue-green with diagonal stripes down the centre.

124 Long knob glazed bright yellow and brown down one side, with a crown and 'H' and foliage.

Hurst Type C–V. Chafing dishes with rectangular medallions. A total of 4.

125 Rectangular knob, with overall pale green tinged cream glaze, depicting a face with a halo or schematic hair. Random splashes of green and yellow on the face but with the features picked out in brown.

126 A rectangular knob outlined either side with 'ladders'. A crudely executed head in the centre with schematic hair/halo. Painted green and yellow with brown detail as in no 125 (above).

Hurst Type C–VI. Chafing dishes with round knobs. A total of 4.

Hurst Type C–VIII. Polychrome arcade. Total of 1. Chafing dish base. Total of 1.

Polychrome Handles
16 handles.

127 Large handle, glazed yellow with brown drips. The interior of the vessel is glazed in yellow-green.

128 Decorated handle in the form of a figure in bed confined around the head; or possibly representing a baby strapped in a sling for carrying on the back. The bed or sling has crudely scored horizontal and wavy lines with splashes of brown, green and cream.

Mottled Polychrome
Vessels generally burnished or wiped towards the base and on the exterior. 3 rims, 1 sherd.

129 Small bowl with a largely unglazed exterior. The interior is glazed pale yellow with random blotches of pale green and brown over a white slip. This vessel has a very broad lug(?) projecting from the outside rim of the vessel (*cf* fig 2, no 3, p.105, Fanning and Hurst, 1975).

Miscellaneous Polychrome
2 unusual decorated knobs; 1 base of candlestick(?) with glaze deteriorated; 1 figurine; 1 unusual ram's head; 17 sherds.

130 Decorative knob(?) with a collar beneath a hole and bead rim. Similar to a whistle but with a wide mouth. Glazed in brown, green and yellow.

131 Part of decorative knob(?) similar to 27.

132 Moulded strip from figurine, glazed bright yellow and brown outside, yellow glazed interior.

Marbled Slip
Clear yellow glazed on the interior but with green-brown marbling on the exterior. 2 rims, 2 sherds.

133 Small handled jug with plain upright rim internally and externally glazed cream with some green flecks. The exterior is marbled with large brown-grey areas. Another similar vessel has 'combed' marbling on the exterior surface.

Saintonge Brown
1 brown glazed handle.

SOUTH WEST FRENCH (Figs 20–21)

Green and brown, 16th and 17th century

Fabric: Pink to buff fine fabric with red inclusions similar to Saintonge. Decorated with blue-green and manganese abstract designs. Some sherds have a slip while others are unslipped. The unslipped pieces, however, have the same opaque appearance as those with a slip. This may be due to the fact that many of the unslipped sherds have a white external margin.

Plates/Dishes

Flanged rims, flat bases, generally burnished on exterior lower half of vessel. 4 rims; 4 bases; 6 sherds.

134 Flanged rim from unslipped dish with deep groove at inside edge of rim. Decorated with a green wavy line.

135 Flanged dish with manganese and green decoration on the rim.

136 Base of a plate speckled blue with blue-green lines at centre.

137 Two sherds showing style of decoration consisting of blue arcs with hatched infilling and splashes of green glaze.

Bowls

1 rim; 1 base; 4 sherds.

138 Rim inturned slightly with traces of handle/lug broken off externally at the rim. The interior has pale green horizontal stripes and manganese decoration beneath, which is infilled with blurred green hatching. The exterior is rather burnt but is glazed. (*cf* no 1094, Platt and Coleman-Smith 1977).

139 Base of vessel burnished outside at base with interior decoration outlined in manganese and filled with close horizontal green stripes.

Jugs/Jars

140 Globular jar with bead footring in a soft pale pink fabric with numerous opaque red, white and black inclusions. A speckled green glaze covers the exterior of the vessel only. Possibly from the Saintonge.
See Table 6 for quantities.

MISCELLANEOUS WHITE (Fig 21)

Fabric: Generally typical of south France and Saintonge, although there are some variants which are coarser and/or micaceous. Some sherds seem to be earlier than the broad post-medieval context: for example, the spout of a medieval jug. See Table 6 for quantities.

141 Jar in a white fabric, green glazed on the interior, with a concave rim from which a broad strap handle springs. Round the neck and running beneath the handle is an horizontal applied thumb/finger impressed strip. Probably South-West French.

MISCELLANEOUS FRENCH (Fig. 21–22)

17th century

142 Almost complete narrow necked jar with a groove on the shoulder and a square footring. Fine red micaceous sandy fabric with a red slip still visible at the base. Overall dark green glaze inside and outside. Possibly North French origin, 17th century.

143 Costrel in red fabric and green glazed with spout. Beneath the spout is a stamped applied square medallion with floral motifs. At one end is a circular medallion depicting a bird. Possibly North French. First half of 17th century.

144 Loire type jug in a hard creamy-white micaceous fabric with possible traces of glaze. The handle springs directly from the rim at a point opposite the pouring lip. In medieval times the form was slightly different. On present distribution these are more commonly found in Northern England and Scotland (fig 4, 5, p 206, Dunbar and Hay 1960–61) than in Southern England (fig 11, 11, p 36, Maynard 1969). 16th or 17th century.

BEAUVAIS STONEWARE (Fig 22)

17th century

Beauvais stoneware was produced as early as the 14th century and continued into the 19th century.

Fabric: Grey to cream stoneware with sporadic patches of pale green-grey glaze.

Costrels

With slight collar on neck, deep grooves at shoulder, and transverse strap handles. 1 rim, 1 sherd.

145 Collared neck and rim of costrel with a patch of glaze on the grooved shoulder.

146 Grooved sherd from the shoulder of a costrel with the base of a transverse strap handle.

Jars

1 rim.

147 Everted rim of a glazed jar with a deep groove on the neck.

Jugs

1 rim; 4 handles.

148 Rim and handle of a jug with patchy glaze.

Miscellaneous

4 bases; 4 sherds.

149 Base of vessel glazed pale green-grey externally. Prominent throwing rings on interior. Turned-up outer edge at base.

MARTINCAMP STONEWARE FLASKS
16th century

The origin of the flasks, unknown until recently, is now assigned to Martincamp as a result of the 1974 drainage scheme (Hurst, 1977a). J G Hurst has divided these flasks into three types which range from the 15th to the 17th century (Hurst, 1966).

> *Hurst Type II.* Stoneware, 16th century. Some sherds have patches of glaze and they span a range of colours.
> 4 sherds from the front of a flattened flask; 2 neck sherds; 8 miscellaneous sherds.

NORMANDY STONEWARE (Fig 22)
17th century

Stoneware production in Normandy, North-West France, began in the 14th century, with the main centre at Ger, and it continues up to the present day. Its uniform typology makes it very difficult to date (Barton, 1977) but a 17th century date for this group is most likely.

Fabric: Usually purple-brown stoneware with black margins and brown or black external surfaces, often glazed brown. Underfired, unfused vessels have a grey fabric.

Jugs
3 rims; 3 handles.

150　Jug of grey fabric with purple specks on the interior and patches of brown glaze on the exterior. Thick everted rim stamped with rosettes in the region of the handle, which springs from the apex of the rim.

151　Very fine vessel with everted concave rim and a rilled body. The base of the handle can be seen on the edge of the rim.

Jars
3 rims.

152　Part of a small jar with pouring lip pinched out from rim. Glazed on exterior.

153　Neck and rim of small jar with bead rim, predominantly grey.

154　Simple rim and neck of jar, not fully fused.

Costrels
1 rim.

155　Rim and neck from costrel with patchy glaze on interior and exterior surfaces.

Bases
3 bases.

156　Large flat base with brown-orange glaze on interior and exterior. Probably from storage vessel similar to 47 and 48. (*cf* no 1071 Platt and Coleman-Smith 1977.)

Miscellaneous Sherds
37 sherds, including one with combed wavy line decoration.

GERMANY

NIEDERRHEINISCH (Fig 23)
c1700

This ware was produced at various sites on the lower Rhine, especially at Krefeld. Only imports of coarse examples of the late 17th to early 18th century survive. (Sholten-Neess and Jüttner, 1971.)

Fabric: Fine red sandy fabric with numerous multicoloured inclusions, notably opaque white ones. White slip cut through to reveal red fabric with an overall clear glaze which shows as green/yellow.

157　Two sherds, including base, probably from same vessel. Sgraffito decoration on body consists of pairs of dots cut through slip. Also abstract design with sgraffito outline with green splashes of colour around orange-brown slip decoration.

COLOGNE FRECHEN (Fig 23)
16th–17th century

The earliest manufacture of stoneware at Frechen dates from the beginning or middle of the 15th century. The stoneware potters migrated to Cologne *c*1500 but apparently returned to Frechen in the third quarter of the 16th century. Generally, therefore, it is not possible to distinguish between the products of Frechen and Cologne in this period. There is little evidence of stoneware production in the 18th century, although it was resumed after 1815. (Gobels, 1971; Reineking-von Bock, 1976).

Note: This group of sherds is listed below in two ways. In Part I the material has been divided according to the colour of the interior, which was found to be the most convenient criterion for sorting. This method is not altogether satisfactory as the internal colour can vary on one vessel, especially in the region of the rim. This explains why some colours have no rim sherds. In Part II the same sherds are described in more detail and arranged in groups according to their decorative motifs.

BELLARMINE AND RELATED VESSELS
PART I

Plain grey interior
6 long-necked rims with simple groove; 9 collared rims with shorter neck, 7 of them with handles; 18 bases with cordons, 10 with wire marks; 2 plain bases without cordons; 8 masks, 3 unidentifiable; 9 medallions, 3 unidentifiable; 8 small round medallions with acanthus leaves and inscribed bands.

Red-Pink Interior
3 long-necked rims with groove beneath; 10 collared rims with shorter neck, 4 with handles; 10 bases with cordons, 2 with wire marks; 2 plain bases without cordons; 17 masks; 6 medallions; 1 acanthus leaf etc.; 4 handles; 88 sherds.

Yellow-Orange Interior
25 long-necked non-collared rims, excluding marks and 4 with handles; 3 collared rims with shorter necks, excluding marks and 3 with handles; 23 bases with cordons, 15 with wire marks; 4 bases without cordons, 1 with wire marks; 14 masks; 10 medallions; 3 handled vessels with larger diameter necks and with groove beneath rim and cordon at junction of neck and body; 1 miscellaneous handled vessel.

158 Globular, handled jar with short neck with stamp on neck opposite handle.

Pale Green-Yellow Interior
3 bases with cordons, 2 with wire marks; 2 plain bases without cordons, 1 with wire marks; 4 masks; 3 medallions; 2 acanthus leaves etc.

Grey Interior Speckled White or Yellow with a Concentration of Colour along Throwing Lines
2 tall neck rims; 7 bases without cordons; 10 masks; 59 miscellaneous sherds.

Pink-Grey Interior
1 base without cordon; 1 sherd.

Pink-Buff Interior
159 Miniature bottle with groove beneath rim.

Pink-Orange Interior
1 base without cordon; 5 sherds.

Pink-Brown Interior
1 base without cordon; 1 handle; 1 sherd.

Unglazed Interior
2 bases with cordons; 2 plain bases without cordons; 5 masks, 3 of them unidentifiable; 6 medallions; 2 acanthus leaves etc; 41 sherds.

Oak Leaf and Acorn Decorated Sherds
16th century
4 sherds with oak leaves, stems and acorns; 1 large base with cordon, oak leaves and wire marks (cf no 268, p 204, Reineking-von Bock, 1976).

Miscellaneous
19 rims; 181 handles; 142 sherds.

BELLARMINE AND RELATED VESSELS
PART II

Bellarmine Face Masks
A Summary of Types
First half of 17th century

The decoration of Bellarmine vessels with face masks is part of a long tradition dating from medieval times. They continue well after 1800, although the latest dated Bellarmine example is 1764. Holmes (1951) produced a typological chronology for these vessels, based on the face masks. Although it is useful for distinguishing nine main types, its chronological significance is doubtful. (Thwaite, 1973; Green, J N, 1977).

Holmes Type II. Small neat mouths, surrounded by flowing moustaches and beards. A total of 5, 3 with large faces and beards, 2 smaller ones with hair at the sides of the face, 4 with moustaches flowing down into the beards, and 1 with separate curved-up moustache.

Holmes Type IV. Grinning with palmette beards. Total of 3, all with moustaches.

Holmes Type V. Straight open mouths which show teeth represented by parallel lines with short vertical lines. Often with 'frown' between brows. A total of 4.

160 Straight line of teeth with a beard and a small tuft underneath lower lip. Moustache and whiskers on either side of nostrils. Large eyes with eyebrows. Some lines between eyebrows representing a frown. Nostrils represented by dots.

Mask with straight open mouth and teeth. Prominent lower lip represented by lines. Neat small beard. Moustache. Hair at sides of face. Eyes with eyebrows and eyelashes on lower lids. A mess of lines at top of eyebrows representing hair or frown.

Bottom portion of mask with straight incised lines for beard. Mouth outlined with two lines. Teeth, dots for nostrils. No moustache.

Narrow face. Most of beard missing. Moustache. Dots for nostrils. Teeth. Neat line of twisted hair at side of face.

Holmes Type VII–VIII. Voluted or hour-glass mouth. Total of 7.

161 Large mask, unglazed interior with eyebrows and a long branching frown between the eyes. Dots for nostrils. Hair at sides of face. Open mouth with double outline and pushed-up in the centre of the lower lip. Fangs at side of mouth with cross in the centre. Simple beard with tuft beneath lower lip.

Small beard represented by straight crude lines. Hour-glass mouth with teeth (?fangs) at ends only. No moustache. Dots for nos-

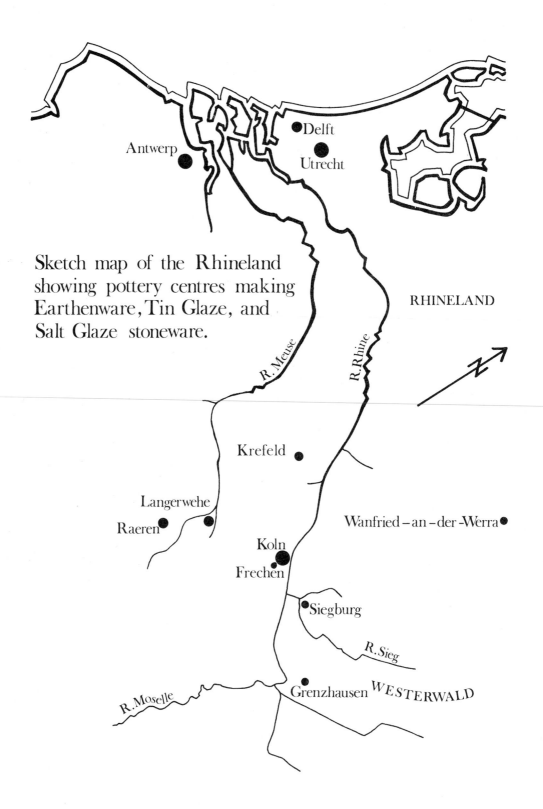

Delft

Antwerp

Utrecht

Sketch map of the Rhineland
showing pottery centres making
Earthenware, Tin Glaze, and
Salt Glaze stoneware.

RHINELAND

R.Meuse

R.Rhine

N

Krefeld

Langerwehe

Wanfried–an–der–Werra

Raeren

Koln

Frechen

Siegburg

R.Sieg

R.Moselle

Grenzhausen WESTERWALD

MAP 4

trils. Lashes on lower eyelids. Hair above eyes (?brows). Vertical lines at top of head.

Hour-glass mouth outlined with two lines. Teeth at ends and tongue in middle. Crude beard with tuft of hair under centre of bottom lip. No moustache. Dots for nostrils. Top of head missing.

Lower half of mask with hour-glass mouth outlined with two lines. Teeth on outside edges of mouth. Small neat beard with tuft under centre of lower lip. Dots for nostrils. No moustache.

Straight line for beard, very crude. Probably hour-glass mouth with dot in corner. Lips outlined with two very crude lines. Dots for nostrils. No moustache.

Lower portion of mask. Dots for nostrils. No moustache. Mouth open and outlined with double line. Teeth at end and ?tongue in middle.

Small crudely formed beard. Open, thick-outlined mouth, probably hour-glass shape. Mouth with teeth in centre. Beard with tuft beneath lower lip.

Unclassified Masks
Total of 33.

Mouth represented by small neat arc. Simple flowing beard from centre with moustache joining it. Dots representing nostrils. Deep groove delineating bottom of eye. Eyelashes/eyebrows. 'T'-shaped lines between eyebrows representing a frown.

Portion of mask showing eyes with eyebrows. Dots for nostrils and two strokes representing part of moustache/whiskers.

Upper portion of small mask. Eyebrows. Twisted hair at side of face. Moustache represented by horizontal lines flowing down into ?beard.

Upper part of mask with hair at top of head. Eyebrows. Hair down right hand side of face. Lines forming V beneath nose and above moustache.

Top of face with two horizontal lines immediately above eyes within which is a band divided with short vertical lines. Hair at sides of face, between eyes mess of lines. Dot for nostril with whiskers attached.

Upper half of mask, rather crudely formed with mess of lines at top of face representing hair or frown or both.

Upper half of mask which is broken below nose. Cross in centre of brows—?frown. Lines for eyebrows. Dots for nostrils.

Upper portion of mask with numerous arched lines over eyes divided with vertical line. Represent ?bushy eyebrows or ?parted hair. Small neat eyes. Dot for nostril. Part of moustache.

Three sherds showing portions of beards only, one with tuft beneath lower lip.

Two sherds similar to above three but with straight strands grouped together in three's.

Sherd with eye and showing hair at side of face.

Sherd showing flowing hair at side of face and part of moustache.

Sherd with eye and eyebrow.

Sherd with ?hair (vertical lines) in two inverted joining arcs above eyes. Scrawl between eyes, at top of nose ?frown.

Portion of face showing part of eyes. Dot for nostril. Moustache.

Sherd with eye and hair at side of face.

Sherd with 'V' shaped frown above eyebrows and eyes.

Sherd with eyes, dots for nostrils.

Top portion of mask. Straight horizontal line at top of head with vertical line with dot at end between eyes. Moulded eyebrows/lashes.

Mask fragment showing hair at sides of face.

Fragment with eye and moulded brow.

Twisted strands of flowing beard.

Part of eyebrows with cross between eyes.

Eyelashes/brows with slanting eyes and cross between brows. Dots for nostrils.

Eyes. Moustache.

Very indistinct features. Squashed eyes and nose on small mask.

Eyebrows/lashes and frown.

Two masks with only part of eye and with eyelashes, unglazed inside.

Eyes with dots for brows/lashes. Hair at sides. Dots for nostrils. Mouth missing.

Acanthus Leaves, Inscribed Bands and Small Portrait Medallions

Second half of 16th century. Total of 22. (*cf* Reineking-von Bock, 1976, nos 284, 285.)

Three large sherds from same vessel with acanthus leaves, round medallions and inscribed band: ODEꙄ VERG/ . . . EDR/.

Sherd with small portrait medallion and inscribed band reading/GODES.

Sherd with part of acanthus leaf and inscribed band reading /TEꙄT A.

Large sherd with three others from same vessel. Small medallions. Inscribed band reads /DRINK ∴ EꙄT. GODEꙄ: NIT: VERS/.

Six sherds from different vessels with parts of illegible inscribed bands, acanthus leaves and medallions.

Five sherds from different vessels with parts of acanthus leaves.

Two sherds from different vessels with round portrait medallions.

Two sherds with acanthus leaves and central bands with a running flower and foliage design (Reineking-von Bock, 1976, no 283).

Rim and neck of wide-mouthed jug with portrait medallions on neck (*cf* no 288, Reineking-von Bock, 1976).

Two miscellaneous sherds.

Medallions
A summary. Total of 30.

Seven rosette medallions, one with splashes of blue (*cf* no 266, 274–8, Moorhouse 1970).

Three unidentifiable coats of arms with part of face mask.

One Amsterdam coat of arms (*cf* no 283, Moorhouse 1970).

One small stamped roundel.

One medallion with 'snakey' border.

One elaborate medallion.

Fifteen unidentifiable edges of medallions.

162 Full length figure dressed in slashed breeches and wearing a hat. There is a decorative star between his feet.

163 Heart, crown and rose medallion (*cf* fig 2.1.6. GV 87, p 99–100, Green 1977). The crown depicted here has only three, rather than four, 'jewels'.

164 Two medallions with two inverted fleur-de-lis joined together.

LANGERWEHE
First half of 16th century

Langerwehe lies on the northern border of the Eifel River in the Duchy of Julich. The first production of true stoneware was around the middle of the 14th century, and in this and in the following century it became one of the major centres of stoneware production. However, as it did not develop a fine decorated phase in the 16th century it became eclipsed by other German stoneware centres. Pottery is still made at the Uhlhaus pottery (Hurst, 1977b).

Fabric: Ranges from hard-fired earthenware to a grey stoneware. Various interior surface treatments and exterior glazes are present (Blockley, 1978, p 206–11).

Jugs
4 rims.

Slight groove beneath rim. Grey with patchy bronze-brown on exterior and lustrous bronze glaze on interior.

Plain rim, brown glazed exterior, grey interior.

Two broad grooves beneath rim. Dark brown exterior and matte grey interior.

Collared rim glazed brown outside and matte yellow-brown inside.

Cups
1 rim.

Rim from cup with grey external glaze with patches of brown and lustrous brown glaze on the interior.

Miscellaneous
2 bases with frilled feet and five miscellaneous bases; 22 rilled sherds; 3 shoulder sherds, 2 with splashes of glaze inside; 17 miscellaneous sherds; three sherds from one vessel, underfired, lustrous pale bronze glaze outside and unglazed orange inside.

RAEREN (Fig 23)
First half of 16th century

At some time in the 15th century a stoneware industry was established at Raeren, just south of Aachen. The industry flourished during the first half of the 16th century, with drinking mugs as the most popular item for export. Brown glazed panel jugs were made in the last quarter of that century. In the 1580s cobalt blue was added to the decoration. At the end of the century most of the potters moved to the Westerwald and developed the blue decoration. The Raeren industry, however, continued well after 1632 (Hurst, 1964; Hurst, 1967; Reineking-von Bock, 1976).

Fabric: Grey stoneware usually with lustrous grey or brown or patchy grey-brown glaze.

Mugs/Jugs
(*cf* nos 252–57, p 73–4, Moorhouse, 1970.)
7 rims; 3 handles; 7 bases, 3 of them frilled.

Neck and rim with shoulder and handle base of a mug. Light grey outside with patches of lustrous bronze on rim and neck. Unglazed green-grey interior speckled buff-yellow with a concentration of buff-yellow along some throwing lines.

Rim with handle. Shiny grey glaze with patches of bronze outside. Shiny brown-orange inside.

Rim and neck with handle base of mug. Patchy lustrous grey to bronze colour outside. Shiny brown-orange inside.

Four collared, bevelled rims. Yellow-brown inside and outside.

Ribbed handle. Patchy bronze-grey outside.

Sherd from mug with handle base and part of cordon at bottom of neck. Grey with a few patches of brown outside. Buff with lines of pink inside

Handled sherd from mug, broken at neck. Simple strap handle. Shiny grey outside with a few specks of brown. Light brown-grey interior.

Frilled base. Lustrous grey inside and brown outside. Underfired.

Frilled base. Grey-brown inside. Purple-brown outside.

Frilled base fragment.

Five miscellaneous bases, three of them frilled.

Miscellaneous
1 medallion; 1 shoulder; 1 neck; 1 ?lid; 3 sherds.

165 Unusual elaborate ?lid. Grey outside, pink-brown inside.

Shoulder sherd with cordon on bottom of neck. Mostly lustrous bronze outside with some patches of grey. Unglazed inside green-grey.

Coat of arms medallion depicting rampant lion with crown above. Lustrous dimpled grey outside with green-yellow tinge. Yellow-orange inside.

Neck sherd with rilling. Lustrous grey with patches of bronze outside. Interior unglazed dark grey with orange wash concentrated along throwing lines.

Three miscellaneous body sherds.

Jugs (probably Raeren)
Late 16th to early 17th century
Grey Inside, Bronze-Brown Outside
8 rims, 2 with handles, 1 without cordons; 12 bases; 1 handle; 2 sherds with honeycomb decoration; 12 flutings with decorative panels and decorated cordons; 4 decorative panels.

Vessel with 'gentlemen soldiers' under arches (cf no 424d, p 270, Reineking-von Bock, 1976).

Sherd from an Electors' jug depicting one of the bishops.

Two miscellaneous decorative panel sherds, one with people.

Bronze-Brown Inside, Grey-Blue Outside
3 bases; 2 decorative panels; 6 flutings, 2 with decorative panels; 2 face medallions on neck; 3 rosette medallions; 15 sherds, 3 of them decorated.

Decorative panel on large portion of an Electors' jug with four of the electors represented: the Bishop of Mainz; the Holy Roman Emperor (Rudolf II, 1567–1612); Count Palatinate of the Rhine; and the Duke of Saxony (cf no 427, and pl 30, Reineking-von Bock, 1976). Dated to sometime in the seventeenth century as '16' appears at the base of one of the arches. See also no 166 of this report.

Decorative panel sherd with figures under double arch. One figure appears to be marked.

Brown-Bronze Inside and Outside
1 rim with cordons at base of neck; 1 base; 3 decorative panels; 2 sherds with honeycomb decoration; 15 flutings, 3 with decoration between; 14 sherds.

166 Part of an Electors' jug depicting three of the Electors: the Count Palatinate of the Rhine, the Duke of Saxony, and the Elector of Brandenburg. 03 appears near the base of one of the arches, dating the sherd 1603 (cf no 427, and pl 30, Reineking-von Bock, 1976).

Two vessels with peasant wedding scenes, one with couples dancing under arches. Both have inscribed bands, one above the figures, the other below.

One sherd with part of unidentifiable coat of arms.

Unusual base with flutings. Bronze-brown outside, glazed yellow-green on inside. Wire marks on base.

?RAEREN/?LANGERWEHE
First half of 16th century

In the 15th century most of the stoneware imports came from Langerwehe, with only a few from Siegburg. From the late 15th century an increasing quantity of Raeren vessels were imported which seem to supplant those from Langerwehe by the early 16th century. At this time many of the products are similar in appearance, so that it is often difficult to distinguish between them.

Jugs: Summary
8 rims; 8 bases with frilled feet; 3 shoulders; 11 miscellaneous sherds, 9 of them with rilling; 2 handles.

Jugs: Detail
Rim with lustrous speckled brown glaze outside. Rilled neck. Orange glaze inside.

Rim with rilling outside. Patchy green-grey outside, brown-yellow inside.

Two rim sherds. Lustrous grey with patches of bronze. Rilled outside, unglazed inside, brown with orange specks.

Rilled neck rim sherd. Grey with bronze patches outside. Lustrous bronze inside.

Rim sherd. Pale grey outside and inside with patches of brown. Rilled outside.

Rim sherd. Pale grey outside. Few specks of brown. Rilled. Red-brown inside.

Rim sherd. Yellow-brown inside and outside.

Base sherd. Frilled foot. Shiny grey glaze outside with glazed orange-brown interior.

Base sherd. Lustrous bronze with patches of grey outside. Unglazed dark grey inside with specks and concentrations of buff-yellow. Lustrous bronze under base.

Shoulder sherd. Lustrous grey with patches of bronze outside. Pink-grey inside.

Shoulder sherd. Rich dark brown outside. Rilled. Red-brown inside.

Shoulder sherd. Not properly fired. Pale mottled brown outside. Unglazed pink inside.

Large sherd with handle base, very crudely attached. Grey outside with a few brown specks and patches. Rilled. Inside unglazed brown with specks of orange.

Transverse handle stump. Green-brown outside. Unglazed grey inside.

Two miscellaneous handles.

SIEGBURG (Fig 23)
Second half of 16th century

The earliest Siegburg salt-glazed stoneware can be assigned to the 14th century. The industry continued into the 17th century with a severe setback in 1632, when the town was sacked during the Thirty Years War, which caused a decline in the pottery production (Klinge, 1972).

Fabric: Creamy-white stoneware often clear-glazed on the exterior.

Jugs
2 rims with handles, 1 of them with rilling; 2 frilled bases of late 15th–early 16th century; 1 handle.

Miscellaneous
1 base with flutings; 11 sherds with flutings and decorative scrolls above panels of cross-hatching; 7 miscellaneous sherds.

167 Medallion from large vessel, clear-glazed externally, showing the profile of Hercules in his war helmet. The portrait is surrounded by an ornamental border. Late 16th–early 17th century (*cf* no 492, Klinge, 1972).

SELTZER BOTTLES

There are four sherds from 19th century seltzer bottles including one unidentifiable stamp (Wittop Koning, 1976).

WESTERWALD (Fig 24)
17th century

Westerwald is the name given to the area lying between the Rivers Sieg and Lahn, east of the Rhine. In the late 16th century, potters from Siegburg and Raeren moved to the Westerwald to join the native potters from Grenzhausen and Hohr. Cobalt blue decoration had already been used by the Raeren potters and continued in use until the third quarter of the 17th century when manganese purple was added. This ware was manufactured well into the 18th century and is, in fact, still produced today (Reineking-von Bock, 1976).

For convenience this group has been divided by decorative technique. This may have some chronological significance, as the pieces with incised decoration only seem to be a little later.

Fabric: Grey or cream-coloured stoneware decorated in blue and sometimes in purple on the exterior.

INCISED
Curvilinear with abstract foliage.

Tankards
Small tankard in cream stoneware with a manganese band at the base and incised foliage above.

Jugs
Globular jug with blue foliage and flower decoration interspersed with close-set zig-zag.

Base of jug with foliage decoration.

Decorated Sherds
Miscellaneous Foliage—1 rim; 10 sherds.

Chevrons and Circles—2 chevrons; 2 sherds with circles.

Floral Surrounded by Zig-Zag—3 sherds.

Geometric—1 rim and 2 sherds with vertical lines; 1 base and 2 sherds chequered; 1 base and 3 sherds lozenged.

Spirals—1 rim; 1 base; 1 sherd.

Miscellaneous Incised
1 rim; 3 bases; 32 sherds.

INCISED AND STAMPED
Curvilinear incised stems and stamped flowers/buds (*cf* nos 506, 577, Reineking-von Bock, 1976).

Tankards
168 Tankard with a central band of typical scroll flower design. The blooms are picked out in manganese.

169 Large tankard base with a stamped AR medallion and incised stylised leaves. First quarter 18th century (*cf* no 545 with a G R medallion; Reineking-von Bock, 1976).

Jugs
170 Globular jug with manganese rilled neck and sprigged design (similar to no 163 of this report) on the body.

Jug with a medallion of William on a horse. Second half of 17th century.

Miscellaneous
5 rims, 2 of them manganese, 1 blue and manganese; 15 sherds, 8 of them blue and manganese.

STAMPED
Jugs
Total of 7.

Globular handled jug with lozenges, hearts and ovals stamped in blue and manganese. Late 17th to early 18th century.

Base of large ovoid jug stamped with manganese hearts surrounded with dots and blue areas.

Twenty sherds with heart and dot decoration in blue and manganese.

Panel jugs
Total of 5.

Two sherds with a frieze of classical figures in oval medallions bearing inscriptions around the edges which depict the virtues. One has a woman with a dog and two children in the background. She is GLAVB or Faith (*cf* no 464, 465, Reineking-von Bock, 1976).

Three sherds with peasant wedding scenes. One date 1597.

MISCELLANEOUS VESSELS

Flowers in Bunches or Vases—1 base; 3 sherds (*cf* no 519, Reineking-von Bock, 1976).

Lozenges with Roundels Inside—13 sherds.

Bryony—3 sherds.

Scaly Decoration (squamiform)—3 sherds, representing 3 different vessels. (*cf* no 551 Reineking-von Bock, 1976).

Lozenges with Acorns Inside—1 sherd.

Cross-Hatching—11 sherds.

Floral—1 rim; 1 base; 6 sherds.

Faces—3 sherds.

Panel Decoration—5 sherds, 1 of them with bird, 1 with animal.

Cock—1 sherd.

Miscellaneous Stamped—50 sherds.

Flutings
The usual basal variety. Some interspersed with incised hearts and circles, herringbone decoration, or pillars of raised dots.

12 flutings interspersed by heart and circle; 15 plain flutings; 1 base and 2 sherds of herringbone flutings; 1 base and 2 sherds of flutings interspersed by pillars of raised dots; 4 flutings interspersed by miscellaneous decoration; one sharply carinated handled jar with decorated cordons and flutings.

Medallions
5 unidentifiable.

Chamber Pots
9 rims; 8 bases; 15 sherds.

Handles
35, 1 is twisted and many have holes bored into the top.

Spouts
5 with heavy moulding.

Seltzer Bottle Marks
3 marks.

Miscellaneous
36 rims, including 12 with handles; 13 tankard bases; 15 jug bases; 59 cordoned sherds, 21 of them decorated cordons; 96 sherds.

WANFRIED (Figs 24–25)
Late 16th to early 17th century

Wanfried slipware was made at Wanfried-an-der-Werra and Witzenhausen which lie on the flood plain of the river Werra south-east of Kassel. It was produced in the late 16th and 17th centuries and there are many dated examples which range from 1575 to 1632. It was traded in large quantities to Bremen, Leeuwarden, Rotterdam and Great Britain. Wanfried slipware was also taken to Jamestown, Virginia by the first British settlers (Hurst, 1972; Naumann, 1974).

Fabric: Fine red sandy fabric with opaque white/pink inclusions. A white slip design is covered with an overall clear glaze giving a pale green design on a brown background. Sgraffito outline and detail to design. Dashes on the rim.

Plates
Plates have hammer-headed rims and external rilling.
Continuous Scroll Border—7 rims; 1 base.

171 Complete profile of a plate with ornate continuous scroll border decoration.

172 Rim of plate with oblique strokes at the rim and continuous scroll border.
Scroll and Stroke Border—5 rims; 1 base; 7 sherds.
Ornamental Arc Border—(*cf* p 29, J Naumann 1974) 6 rims; 2 sherds.

173 Complete profile of plate with ornamental arc border.

Large Decorated Sherds
Anthropomorphic—3 sherds.

174 Base of dish depicting sgraffito outlined man with sgraffito detail (e.g. buttons and hair). The upper half of the man is very pale green and he has green trousers. The sherd is dated . . . 6 . . . 11 (1611).

175 Base from smaller dish depicting a man's legs with a hand holding a leaf/flower over his posterior. The decoration is pale green with occasional darker tinges. The '2' of a date appears, representing a date sometime in the 1620s.
Human head date . . . 18 (1618).
Fishes—3 bases, 1 sherd.

176 Complete profile of vessel with hammer-head rim, depicting three interlocking green-glazed sgraffito fishes. Plain concentric line border.

177 Dish/bowl depicting a large fish in pale and some dark green. External rilling. '1' from a date.
Animals—3 sherds.

178 Small sherd with an animal head on the interior and external rilling.

179 Sherd depicting a dog-like animal with a snout, ears and paws and a bow around the neck.

180 Animal head with ?horns. Dated ... 20 (1620.)

Fragmentary Dates
1 rim; 2 bases showing fragments of dates which cannot be definitely assigned.

Miscellaneous
8 rims; 14 bases; 30 sherds.

Cups or Bowls
Usually with external rilling.
14 rims, 5 of them with handles or handle scars; 2 bases from complete profiles.

181 Complete profile of bowl with external rilling and a transverse handle. Dashes painted on the outside edge of rim. Plain concentric line border with a sgraffito outline.

182 Sherd with sgraffito feet overlapping the scroll and stroke border design. External rilling.

WESER (Fig 25)
Second half of 16th to early 17th century

Weser slipware was made at the potteries of Southern Lower Saxony in the 'Pottland' between the rivers Weser and Leine. Two production centres so far identified are at Coppengrave and Völksen, near Hanover. The ware has a date range from the second half of the 16th century to the mid-17th century, with some continuation until c1770. For a time Weser slipware seems to have been one of the most important German ceramics for export (G Stephan, forthcoming).

Fabric: Pink fabric with multicoloured inclusions and hairline fissures, with a thin white slip inside over which has been applied a trailed slip design in green and brown. An overall clear glaze gives a yellow background.

Plates
Basically with hammer-headed rims and flat bases. All vessels are burnished on the lower half of the exterior. 31 rims; 10 bases; 27 sherds.

183 These sherds could be reconstructed to
184 represent a typical plate with a zone beneath
185 the rim consisting of two thin brown lines either side of a broad band, delineating the upper part of an area decorated with alternate green and brown wavy lines grouped together in fours. Thick and thin lines also form the bottom boundary to this decoration, beneath which is a very slight internal ridge and a plain undecorated zone with thick and thin lines below it. The central motif consists of further alternate brown and green

wavy lines radiating out from the centre in pairs. These sherds are, in fact, from three different vessels as can be demonstrated by the variation in the thickness of the lines. The underside of the bases may have wire marks.

186 Rim of plate with concentric thick and thin line border decoration. The zone beneath is decorated with interlocking brown and green m's or n's (?) interspaced with wavy lines.

187 Carinated plate with unusual decoration. Two thin brown lines at the rim with a broad zone beneath consisting of brown circles with brown blotches in the centre with sporadic green dots at the edge. These are interspersed with six (?) oblique brown strokes crossed by green ones. There are 4 concentric lines near the base which are traversed by a yellow wavy line. Concentric thick and thin line border. *cf* Leiden example from Van Beuningen collection in G Stephan (forthcoming).

Decorated Sherds—Multiple Concentric Line Border—18 rims; 17 bases.

Panels of Wavy Lines—Usually grouped in 2s, 3s or 4s in alternate colours. 50 sherds.

Panels of Alternately Coloured Dots—8 sherds.

Miscellaneous
28 rims; 30 sherds.

Carinated Bowls
Total of 9.

188 Bowl with multiple concentric line border decoration at the rim, beneath which is a band of alternate green and brown wavy lines.

189 Carinated bowl with yellow strokes at the rim and multiple yellow lines on the interior. External ridges above the carination.

190 Bowl with slight carination and wire marks at base. The decoration at the centre consists of alternate green and brown wavy lines grouped in 4s.

Handles
Total of 5.

191 Handle from jug with dot decoration.

Miscellaneous
1 sherd with wavy lines on exterior, possibly from a jug.

Pipkins
Total of 2.

192 Rim of pipkin glazed brown-ochre on the interior. Pale yellow exterior with alternate green and brown dashes on rim and alternate green and brown vertical stripes over rouletting.

ITALY

MONTELUPO TIN GLAZE (Figs 26–27)
Second half 16th to first half 17th century

Montelupo is a small town in the Arno Valley between Florence and Pisa. Kilns here are thought to have supplied Florence with some of the finest maiolica in the 15th century, although simpler wares were produced for export. Montelupo was the main centre for export wares, and there are very few examples from other factories in north West Europe (Procacci, 1973).

Fabric: Buff to pinky-red soft chalky fabric with very minute red and darker inclusions. An opaque white tin glazed exterior, usually with horizontal manganese bands. Frequently has brightly coloured designs inside.

Dishes
With flat wire-marked bases and generally some rilling on exterior. 19 rims; 18 bases; 30 sherds.

193 Dish with typical geometric design on inside and three rather crude manganese bands round the exterior.

194 Base with alternate green, brown and white chequers at the centre. There is a surrounding zone of coloured ovals interspersed with oblique strokes.

195 Two bases with rosette decoration at centre.
196

Dishes
Large Foliage Designs—16 rims; 8 bases.

197 Dish with internal large foliage decoration consisting of large green leaves interspersed with pale blue dots, swags and orange blobs and brown (manganese) outlines, yellow circles. Wire marks on base.

Dishes
Small Foliage Designs—5 rims; 2 bases; 29 sherds.

198 Complete profile of dish with internal decoration of small foliage and ?fruit with green leaves and with manganese swirls and orange striped yellow fruit. The exterior is plain tin glazed with pale manganese horizontal stripes. Blue circles surround the inside edge of the rim.

199 Larger version of no 198 (above) with slightly larger foliage.

Dishes
Abstract floral designs in yellow and manganese with orange ?fruit. 9 rims; 2 bases; 4 sherds.

200 Base sherd with zones of abstract floral decoration delineated by manganese horizontal lines, with a zone of oblique ovals interspersed with three short manganese strokes. Upper part of vessel decorated with arcs. External manganese band.

201 Rim from dish similar to no 200 (above) with orange strokes and blobs in manganese arcs infilled with manganese swags.

Jugs
Undecorated on interior which is either unglazed or plain tin glazed. 3 rims glazed on interior; 2 bases; 7 sherds.

202 Jug with unglazed interior but tin glazed exterior with abstract green, yellow, yellow-ochre and pale blue design with manganese details. Wire marks on base.

203 Jug which appears to be tin glazed on the interior (at the rim, at least) although it has deteriorated in places. The exterior has abstract decoration painted in manganese, green, pale blue and yellow ochre.

204 Base of jug with plain tin glazed interior, with zonal decoration in blue, yellow and oblique black strokes on the exterior.

205 Tin glazed handle from jug with pale green vertical streaks on the outside.
Tuscan jug with trefoil mouth (Procacci, 1973, p 13–14).

Vessel Decorated on Interior and Exterior. These are open vessels and are possibly deep bowls. 11 rims; 11 basal; 40 sherds including 6 with cordons and 6 with foliage on both surfaces.

206 Two very similar rim sherds decorated on
207 both the inside and the outside with a blue band covering the apex of the rim. Both vessels have yellow ochre painted fish/animal heads on the interior with manganese flourishes and a yellow band round the inside of the rim. One rim has some green paint on the outside.

208 Basal sherd. The interior has abstract decoration in horizontal zones. The exterior has a blue background with yellow and yellow ochre blobs, and swirls cut through to the white slip. Five sherds.

209 Part of a deep-sided bowl with an external groove. Random floral decoration appears on the exterior and interior surfaces. The interior has large green leaves outlined in manganese with an overlapping spiked yellow ochre flower and interspersed with a smaller flower with manganese stamen. Random blue flourishes occur throughout. The exterior has the same yellow ochre and smaller flowers but the spiked flower overlaps a yellow leaf (*cf* fig 66, 3, Barton, 1964).

210 Small sherd from ?bowl with restrained decoration on the interior of blue wavy lines and simple zonal decoration with part of a ?central motif of green and yellow buds on blue ?stalks. Oblique painted blue lines on the exterior.

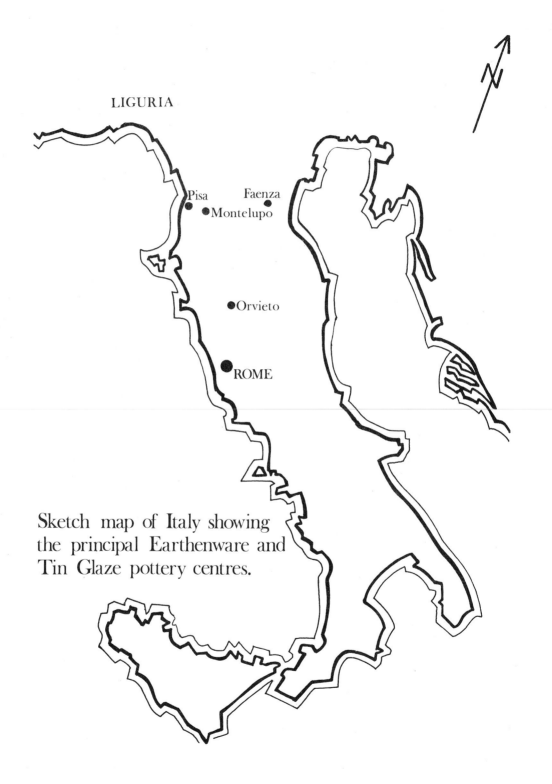

LIGURIA

Pisa   Faenza

Montelupo

Orvieto

ROME

Sketch map of Italy showing
the principal Earthenware and
Tin Glaze pottery centres.

MAP 5

211 Blue leaf design on interior and exterior surfaces, outlined and detailed in manganese. On each side the leaf is halved having one side pale and the other dark blue. Three sherds.

Pedestal Bases
These probably belong to the same category of vessel as the 'deep-sided' bowls. Total of 4 bases.

212 Stepped pedestal base with alternating bands of blue and yellow ochre. Plain tinglazed on the underside. The interior is decorated in blue and green with some manganese flourishes.

Cavalier Pattern Plates
With solid blocks of colour—3 rims; 3 bases; 2 sherds.

213 Rim from cavalier plate decorated with solid blocks of blue, green, yellow and yellow ochre with some manganese detail.

Miscellaneous
8 rims; 37 sherds, 2 of them fluted, 1 carinated and 1 moulded.

FAENZA TIN GLAZE

2 bases.

Tin glazed base sherd stained copper green and painted in blue. *c*1680.

Base with mark on underside of base of a circle of three discontinuous lines with dots along one line and a crudely painted cross in the centre (*cf* p 216, MacDonald-Taylor, 1976).

LIGURIA TIN GLAZE

1 basal sherd.

Basal sherd of blue painted white tin glaze with mark on underside showing the Pharos of Genoa. First quarter of 18th century (*cf* p 276, MacDonald-Taylor 1976).

NORTH ITALIAN MARBLED (Fig 28)
First half of 17th century

Marbled ware was probably made in several North Italian centres. Wasters of bowls, but not costrels, have been found in Pisa. Green marbling also seems to have been made in the area of Antibes in the south of France, but it is more likely that all the Plymouth examples come from the Pisa area (Hurst, 1967).

Fabric: Fine red sandy fabric with minute inclusions and some hairline fissures. A predominantly white marbled slip is applied to the surface and the whole vessel is then covered with a clear glaze. The marbling is usually of the 'combed' type but there are some 'blotched' examples.

Bowls
If clear glazed on the exterior they are often unglazed toward the base, and often have grooves on the exterior.

Black and white marbling inside and out. 1 rim; 1 base; 8 sherds.

Black and white marbling outside, with the addition of green inside. 7 rims; 6 bases; 21 sherds.

Plain glazed outside, red and white marbled inside. 36 rims; 8 bases; 30 sherds.

Plain glazed outside; red and white marbled inside. 36 rims; 8 bases; 30 sherds.

Plain glazed outside; black, white and green marking inside. 11 rims, 5 of them with groove along lip. 2 bases; 10 sherds.

214 Bowl with groove along centre of everted rim. Interior marbled with green. Exterior clear lead glaze with fingernail marks at base.

White marbling inside and outside. 4 bases, 2 of them slightly omphalos.

Thinner-walled Bowls. Predominantly white marbling. 2 rims; 1 base; 1 sherd.

Miscellaneous Bowls
9 rims, 2 of them predominantly green; 31 sherds.

Straight-Sided Vessels
With broad bead rim, often with rilling outside and with varying colours of marbling. 7 rims; 43 sherds.

215 Deep, straight-sided bowl with some external rilling. Thick rolled-over bead rim. Marbled internally and externally cream on amber-brown.

216 Bowl similar to no 215 (above) but with undercut everted rim. Marbled interior cream and brown on a predominantly buff background created by an underlying white slip.

Carinated Dishes
Varying colours of marbling. 2 rims; 9 sherds.

217 Carinated dish marbled internally only in cream on amber-brown. External clear lead glaze with groove at external carination.

Small Bowls
With upright plain rims, varying colours of marbling. 16 rims; 2 sherds.

218 Two small plain rimmed bowls. Cream marbling on interior and exterior.
219

Costrels
(*cf* nos 1363, 1364, Platt and Coleman-Smith 1977). Total of 5.

220 Base of costrel with bead footring. External marbling which stops above base. Internal clear glaze. Part of small transverse handle (?lion).

Blotched Marbling
Possibly later or from another source. 1 rim; 3 sherds.

221 Blotched marbled bowl with green tinges. Broad shallow external groove beneath rim.

Miscellaneous Marbled Dishes
Possibly from another source. Not glazed outside, different pattern of marbling. Total of 11 vessels represented.

222 Dish with rim curving inwards and internal ridge at the base. Internal white slip with brown combed marbling splashed with green. No external glaze. Flat base with wire marks.

223 Carinated dish with amber-brown glazed interior with green tinges. Unusual style of marbling with swirls and large blotches. Unglazed rilled exterior. Hammer-head rim.

224 Dish of coarser fabric with white slip marbling and green tinges. Drips of glaze on the exterior.

NORTH ITALIAN SGRAFFITO (Figs 28–29)
First half 17th century

The glaze and fabric is very similar to the marbled wares made at Pisa.

Fabric: Brick red dense fabric with a white slip inside and/or outside, depending on vessel type. Flecked with green and yellow-brown over areas of abstract sgraffito swirls/flowers and covered with an overall clear glaze.

Small Bowls
With plain, almost upright rim. White slipped with horizontal green or yellow bands on the exterior. *cf* North Italian Marbled Small Bowls in this report. 5 rims; 2 bases; 14 sherds.

Carinated Dishes
Clear glazed on exterior. Interior with plain concentric sgraffito lines in groups of three dividing zones which are either undecorated or decorated with abstract sgraffito patterns tinged green and yellow. 3 rims; 9 sherds.

225 Carinated dish with sgraffito decoration confined to a zone by three sgraffito horizontal lines. Vessel becomes concave beneath carination and there is further abstract zonal decoration tinged green and yellow ochre alternately. The central design is of abstract swags.

226 Rim from carinated dish without zonal decoration. Three plain sgraffito lines at rim. Central motif visible but unidentifiable.

227 Carinated dish with simple horizontal sgraffito lines.

Non-Carinated Bowls
With more exaggerated flange. 3 rims; 2 bases.

228 Non-carinated dish with sgraffito lines defining a band of abstract decoration of swags and alternating splashes of green and yellow.

Central motif of stylised flowers also painted yellow and green.

229 Non-carinated dish with swags splashed with green and yellow in two zones and apparently undecorated zone near the base.

230 Base with flower decoration as central motif in green and yellow and a typical abstract zone above.

231 Central motif of large flower in brown and green.

Miscellaneous
9 rims; 5 bases, 3 of them with floral designs; 37 sherds.

232 Dense red fabric with white slip on the interior which has a design cut through and an overall green glaze. The design shows black. The rim is slightly inturned. The exterior has drips of green glaze with some white slip at the rim. Possibly from a different source.

JAPAN
Late 17th century

The Japanese porcelain is of poorer quality than the Chinese, and is painted with purplish-grey-blue designs. The main production centre was Arita.

Plates
2 sherds *c*1650–75.

MIDDLE EAST
PERSIAN EARTHENWARE (Fig 30)

233 Rim and two sherds from small blue and white bowl in a buff sandy fabric. Early 17th century, possibly from Kirman.

MISCELLANEOUS MEDITERRANEAN
16th and 17th century (Fig 30)

Unglazed
Lid of chalky, compact pinky fabric with grey-white core. Micaceous with decayed external slip.

Kicked-up handle in pale creamy-pink fabric. Spanish or Mediterranean.

Sherd of very micaceous rather coarse olive jar type fabric. Smoothed exterior.

Miscellaneous object in micaceous red fabric. Smoothed exterior.

Six miscellaneous jars. ?Spanish.

Sherd in olive jar type fabric. Very micaceous. Part of storage jar?

Buff, slightly micaceous sherd, possibly the neck and shoulder of a costrel.

234 Unusual sherd of olive jar type fabric with white slip outside and brown painted stripes over it.

Tin Glazed

Pinky-red fabric, very micaceous, with tin glaze on the internal surface and ?copper lustre decoration.

Compact, chalky pinky-cream micaceous fabric. Flat base with internal throwing rings. Very deteriorated external glaze with some patches on the interior.

Olive jar type fabric with disintegrated glaze ? internal slip. Flat base.

Coarse pinky-red fabric. Specks of disintegrated glaze.

Lead Glazed

235 Large heavy rim in a rough pale pink fabric with white external margins. Internal pale green-yellow glaze on white ?slip. Bead rim with pulled up horizontal thumb/finger impressed band running around the outside of the neck. Some grooves on the shoulder of the vessel.

Large heavy rim of similar fabric to no 235 (above) with a spotted green-yellow internal glaze and buff-brown external slip. Simple rim with very slight bevel.

Neck of jug in brick red, very micaceous fabric with two very small ridges on the neck and a green external glaze. Some specks on the interior.

Pink core with paler external margins. White external slip with two horizontal bands of yellow and brown.

Part of orange-buff horizontal strip ?beneath what may be a rim.

Horizontal handle in chalky buff-red fabric with external slip and green and yellow glaze.

Chalky-pink fabric with white internal margin and surface which is micaceous and has some specks of glaze. Very disintegrated external green glaze.

236 Part of a possible costrel in dense, slightly micaceous brick red fabric with prominent throwing rings on interior. White slip on the exterior under a patchy green glaze. No slip on lower part of vessel. Transverse loop strap handles. *cf* Italian Marbled Costrels in this report.

Rim with triangular cross-section. Red-orange fabric with internal and external white slip. Clear glaze on the interior and green glazed exterior.

Red fabric with speckled green glaze over a white slip.

Thin, dense, chalky-pinky-white fabric, rather micaceous and with sizeable red inclusions.

Flat base, green external glaze.

Red micaceous fabric with grey core. Base with a white slip on the interior surface and a very deteriorated green glaze.

Base, red micaceous fabric with internal white slip and pale green glaze.

Six miscellaneous glazed rims on white or cream fabric.

Three miscellaneous green glazed rims on pinky-red fabrics with large red inclusions.

Eleven miscellaneous green glazed sherds.

Coarse brick-red fabric with some mica. Transverse handle at carination (*cf* Dutch slip bowls) and white slip on interior with green glaze and green glazed exterior.

237 Red fabric with white inclusions and some mica. Internal white slip with green glaze over moulded spiral decoration. Flat exterior with clear glaze.

238 Pink fabric. Base with footring and green external glaze and yellow/white very deteriorated internal glaze.

Rim of thin-walled plate in red-pink fabric with overall green glaze.

Green and Purple

Fabric: Fine red micaceous sandy fabric with a thick white slip with some strokes of manganese decoration painted over in green. Green decoration in the centre of plate, either spiral or concentric circle decoration. Possibly of Mediterranean origin.

239 Flanged rim with green strokes decoration on rim and spiral at centre. Green strokes seem to be marked out in manganese first.

240 Similar flanged rim no 239 (above) with green band and manganese closely ranged strokes at rim. A band of two green lines towards centre in-filled with manganese dots. Central motif of green probably concentric circles.

Alkaline Glaze

5 sherds of dense red fabric with red and white inclusions. Internal green glaze, external white slip with alkaline glaze (see Glossary).

NETHERLANDS

DUTCH TYPE BROWN GLAZED (Fig 31)
16th and 17th century

It is often difficult to tell whether these coarse wares are Dutch, as Dutch forms were copied and migrant potters worked in England, for example at Exeter. They have a wide date range. (Baart *et al.* 1977, p 226).

Fabric: Fine sandy brick red fabric with clear lead glaze on the interior. Some vessels also glazed externally, while others have drips of glaze.

Colanders
7 rims, 2 of them with feet; 25 sherds.

Pipkins
22 rims.

Rims are concave on the inside, with corresponding external groove and a cordon above a sharp carination. Body generally rilled. Interior and exterior brown-amber glaze (*cf* fig 4, no 53, Moorhouse, 1972).

Dishes
9 rims, including 1 large vessel (no 241); 2 bases. Vessels with evidence of flanged feet and with concave rims hammer-shaped externally. Unglazed exterior, clear amber glaze on interior.

241 One large dish with flanged feet and internal cordon towards base.

Bowls
2 bases, with typical 'Dutch' type footring and plain internal glaze.

Jars
4 flat everted rims.

242 Jar with rilling. Glazed internally and externally.

Miscellaneous
243 Rim of dish with lip.

244 Unusual vessel with plain rim and external rilling on upper part of vessel. Glazed all over. Traces of handle.

245 Large handled jar with rilling on exterior. Glazed all over.

Handles
4 handles, pinched.

DUTCH TYPE GREEN AND YELLOW
Late 16th to early 17th century (Fig 31)

Fabric: Hard white to buff with numerous black, red and opaque white inclusions. Green glazed outside, yellow inside.

Jugs/Jars
3 rims with broken flanges; 2 everted hollow rims; 4 rims with carinations very close to rim; 4 straight rims; 1 decorated rim; 3 bases with Dutch type footring; 1 base with flat bead footring; 9 handles, 2 pinched at top and 2 of transverse type.

246 Rim and pinched handle of small jug/jar. Yellow glazed interior (and just over apex of rim) and green glazed exterior. The interior of the rim is concave. The exterior upper part of the body is corrugated. One side of the handle has a rather crudely stamped chequered motif. The pinched handle, concave rim and corrugated body all indicate Dutch origin.

247 Rim of green and yellow jug/jar with

pinched handle and corrugated body as no 246 (above) but with a plain outward-flaring rim. The corrugations become more pronounced lower down body.

Miscellaneous
9 corrugated sherds, 2 of them carinated; 8 carinated sherds; 45 miscellaneous sherds; 1 pipkin foot.

DUTCH TYPE
GREEN BOWLS AND YELLOW BOWLS

Fabric: Dense red fabric as for Dutch Type Brown Glazed. These bowls are glazed either green or yellow internally over a white slip. They have the typical Dutch footring, as on slipware bowls.

Base sherds, 33. Minimum number of vessels, 30.

NORTH HOLLAND SLIPWARE (Fig 32)
Late 16th to 17th century

North Holland slipware dates from the last quarter of the 16th century to the 17th century, with dated examples between 1573 and 1711. Although there does seem to have been a longer slipware tradition in the Netherlands with the discovery of early 15th century kilns at Utrecht, no production centre has been identified for these later wares (Hurst, Neal, Van Beuningen, 1975).

Fabric: Hard red sandy fabric with minute opaque inclusions and white trailed slip decoration with some green covered by an overall clear glaze.

Bowls
The outline of the slip decoration is scratched onto the surface of the vessel before the slip is applied. Most of the exterior unglazed, except at rim.

Geometric Designs—1 chequered rim; 3 chequered bases and 5 abstract floral bases; 1 handle; 1 cross and circles decorated sherd; 2 chequered sherds.

248 Bowl with rosette in green and yellow trailed slip.

249 Bowl with abstract floral motif in mainly yellow, with some green, trailed slip.

250 Abstract floral motif with green leaves/petals and yellow shoots.

Botanical Designs—1 unidentifiable rim; 3 unidentifiable bases; 3 pine/tulip bases

251 Botanical motif. Heart shape at centre. Most of slip missing.

252 Botanical motif with ?tulip and circle with dots surrounding it in green and yellow trailed slip.

253 Bowl with transverse handle and typical oblique-vertical stroke decoration at rim, with two yellow slip blobs with green patches.

Zoomorphic Designs—Birds: 1 rim, 6 bases, 3 sherds. Peacock: 2 sherds.

Miscellaneous
71 rims; 37 bases; 23 handles; 3 sherds, possibly with parts of dates, not decipherable.

254 Sherd showing a zone of spiral decoration just beneath the missing rim.

Dishes
5 rims.

255 Dish with unglazed exterior. Amber-brown glaze at the rim on the interior and plain green glazed beneath the rim flange. Typical Dutch 'pulled' feet.

256 Similar to no 255 (above) but thinner vessel with a trailed slip design in centre and strokes on the interior of the flange.

Pipkins
Decorated on exterior, plain glazed interior.

257   Two sherds with abstract slip decoration
258   interspersed with green dots. One sherd has a handle base. From separate vessels.

SPAIN

GREEN GLAZED
HEAVY FLANGE DISHES (Fig 33)
17th century

These green glazed dishes are part of a long-standing Mediterranean tradition dating back to the 12th century. It seems likely that they are Spanish (Hurst, 1977c).

Fabric: Pink to buff fine sandy fabric with numerous multicoloured inclusions and fissures with some mica. A white slip has been applied to the exterior and a thick irridescent green glaze to the interior. These vessels have a heavy flange and are similar in form to the Merida vessels of the same type. Most sherds have lines of string marks (either single or double) on the apex of the flange. The largest sherd also has a line of beading inside the rim.

5 rims, 1 without string marks on apex; 1 sherd.

259 Complete profile with internal green glaze and bead inside rim. Unglazed exterior but red painted 'A' on one sherd. Flat rough-finished base with white slip on outside. Crude ?tool marks on outside towards the base.

MERIDA RED (Figs 34–36)
16th or 17th century

The main centre was at Merida in Extramadura in Southwest Spain. In the early period from the late 13th century to early 14th century the range of types was limited to costrels and bottles. More diverse production continued into the 16th century. Similar vessels are still made today in the Alentejo, southern-central Portugal (Parvaux, 1968).

Fabric: Fine micaceous orange-red sandy fabric, with minute opaque white and black inclusions. There is a concentration of micaceous grits on the flat bases of the larger vessel types. Variations in surface treatment occur on different vessel types. The vessels from Castle Street have been analysed by J Evans and fall into three groups:

Group I: Allover black surface deposits. This colouration appears to be a reduced phase of the pottery fabric. It is certainly not a slip nor an independent film of any sort. It contains no organic residues.

Group II: Black patches. These deposits can be sub-divided into a further two groups. The first group appears to have deposits of finely-divided carbon, possibly from 'sooting' during usage or firing. The second group contains traces of wood resins. (Insufficient material was available to attempt any form of classification.) Again, such residues may have been deposited during firing or during usage.

Group III: These residues all have an inorganic nature and appear to be composed mainly of calcium salts with traces of various other elements such as iron. The variations in colour are caused by the variation of the elemental concentrations, especially iron. The deposits were most likely left by water percolating through the pot in the ground.

Globular Lattice Vessels
With burnished or painted-on lattice decoration on exterior over a red slip often dribbled inside. Mostly flat bases slightly omphalos. 16 rims; 19 bases; 65 sherds.

260 Complete profile of vessel with single burnished lattice decoration. Handle springing directly from rim. Throwing rings on interior. Flat base.

261 Red slip with burnished lattice decoration, consisting of single oblique strokes crossed by double strokes.

262 Similar vessel to no 261 (above) but with single stroke lattice design.

263 Rim with two grooves beneath plain rim. Everted funnel neck. Slip on exterior with drips on interior. Crudely painted black-

brown horizontal lines on neck with lattice decoration painted similarly on body.

264   Minute sherd representing either a lid or pedestal base of a small fine vessel.

Heavy Flange Dishes
Always burnished on interior and usually with a heavily micaceous underside of base. 43 rims; 20 bases; 53 sherds.

265   Complete profile of large dish burnished inside and with reduced interior and exterior surfaces.

266   The base of a vessel similar to no 265 (above), burnished in concentric or spiral bands around the interior of the vessel. Smoothed exterior with some horizontal scored marks towards the base. A concentration of mica at the base.

Bowls
With hollow base. Burnished on interior, usually carinated and blackened. Rims vary: some are plain, others with one or more grooves beneath. 154 rims; 49 bases.

267   Carinated vessel burnished inside in spiral/ concentric bands. Groove beneath exterior of rim. Lower half of vessel appears to be sooted. (See note by J Evans.) Kicked-up base with slight tooled groove at the exterior.

268   Similar to no 267 (above) but with carefully flanged rim. Internal burnishing in the usual manner. Slight external surface ridges.

Large Funnel-shaped Jars
All with reduced exteriors. 9 rims, including one smaller version.

269   Thick-walled vessel with very slightly in-turned rim. Smoothed interior, partially reduced, rather uneven reduced exterior with some scored tool marks. (No complete profile for this type.)

Barrel Costrels
With either burnished or painted stripes on exterior. A thin wash of a fine red slip prior to decoration. 7 rims; 13 handles; 2 knobs; 4 sherds.

270   Barrel costrel with external red slip and burnished stripes. Ridge beneath collared neck. Neck concave outside down to the first projecting collar, followed by groove above the second collar. Smoothed interior.

271   Large sherd of barrel costrel, including handle with painted stripes in place of the burnished ones on no 270 (above).

272   Boss from costrel with external slip and burnished to give a smooth surface.

273   Unusual rim and neck from costrel.

Jugs
4 rims; 9 bases, 4 of them non-waisted with vertical burnishing; 6 handles; 291 sherds.

274   Jug with vertical burnishing and collared rim. Slightly collared neck (i.e. slight carination). Crude zig-zag burnished on neck.

The shoulder is accentuated by two grooves. The exterior of the body is decorated by vertical burnished stripes which stop at the waisted base. The stump of a handle is present at a slightly peculiar angle. The underside of the base is very micaceous.

275   Rim of similar form to no 274 (above) but with close vertical burnished stripes beneath the collar.

276   Waisted base with burnished vertical stripes and heavily micaceous base.

277   Non-waisted base from similar vessel type to no 276 (above), also with burnished vertical stripes and heavily micaceous base. Some nail decoration at base.

278   Large plain waisted base. Micaceous underside.

Small Upright Costrels
14 rims.

279   Reduced exterior. Collared neck with slightly oblique burnished stripes. Kicked-up handles. Brick red interior with pull marks at neck.

280   Small, with flanged rim and slight groove above kicked-up handle. External red slip.

281   Small, rather crude collared neck.

Triangular Rims
8 rims.

282   Rims of triangular cross-section with slight
283   ridge beneath.

Miscellaneous Vessels
284   Wide-mouthed jar with three cordons at rim.

285   Unusual, rather crudely-finished rim which in plan has a triangular projecting lip.

286   Large rim sherd of dish with a sharp carination at the shoulder which is accentuated by an underlying groove which tails off. *cf* Merida Bowls.

287   Part of ?shallow dish with decayed external red slip. Groove beneath rim and at shoulder (*cf* Merida bowls.)

288   Vessel with an external red slip and a body indented with evenly spaced rows of hollows beneath a cordon at the bottom of the neck. Base of ?handle.

289   Base of vessel which has been trimmed externally with an internal slight hollow at the centre of the base, with edges of an upper layer of clay surrounding it. Red external slip. Handle base.

290   Part of heavy round-based vessel with hole through centre. From the inside this appears to have been deliberately bored, at least part of the way, although externally this does not seem to be true. The exterior surface is reduced.

291 Unusual base/boss very slightly tooled on exterior to form a flattened circular area. The interior has a dark slip over the prominent throwing rings.

292 Unusual base/boss with internal and external red slip. Flattened outside. Internal throwing rings.

293 Part of ?sagging base with some crude tool marks on exterior at carination. Sooted externally.

294 Micaceous base of vessel with red internal and external slip. External incised decoration infilled with white slip.

295 Vessel with internal incised decoration infilled with white slip. The external surface has been smoothed.

296 Rim with collars at neck beneath which are vertical incised lines crossed with random strokes of white slip.

297 Base of vessel with white painted decoration.

298 Undulating body sherd with abstract incised lines on the exterior surface.

299 Body sherd with burnished area bounded by a shallow groove beneath which is a zone of oblique combed decoration.

300 A decorative, shell-like knob.

301 Basal sherd with pointed cordon at carination, above which are three scored lines which underlie four stamped roundels.

302 Three sherds with external cordons and ver-
303 tical indentations with cordons beneath (or above).

304

305 Rim with moulded 'pie-crust' type decoration.

306 Moulded decoration on rim, slightly concave on the inside.

307 Large heavy handle with slight finger impression on one side. One of two such handles. Possibly from upright costrels.

OLIVE JARS (Figs 36–37)
Late 16th to 17th century

The forms have survived from Roman times, and were produced until well into the 19th century. Attempts, therefore, to form a chronological typology have not proved very successful (Goggin, 1960). The origin of olive jars is unknown, although they are thought to have come from the area around Seville and to have been mainly intended for exporting olives and olive oil. Their distribution is world-wide.

Fabric: There seems to be a great deal of variation in the colouring (terracotta to buff/white) and superficial treatment of olive jars, although on close analysis the fabric is consistently tempered. It is a coarse granular fabric with pre-

dominantly white (but also red and black) inclusions, usually with some cavities and fissures. Frequently there is a thin white slip applied to the exterior surfaces which often have signs of being wiped. Crude tool marks and rillings are quite common on the outside of the vessels. Where the fabric has been imperfectly wedged, bulging and splintering occurs.

Unglazed
14 rims, 4 of them uncollared; 6 curved bases; 1 handle; 423 sherds.

308 Rim, smooth creamy-buff surfaces. Slightly undercut collar on rim.

309 Rim.

310 Rim, flanged, without collar.

311 Rim, smooth creamy-buff surfaces.

312 Rim, slightly hollow on interior.

313 Rim.

314 Unusual olive jar type. Pale cream fabric. Simple rim slightly thickened at top. Rilled body beneath shoulder accentuated by some crude horizontally scored lines. Bulge on surface.

Glazed
Green glazed—4 rims; 51 sherds.

Yellow Glazed—1 rim; 26 sherds.

Green-Yellow Glazed—2 bases; 22 sherds.

Miscellaneous Glazed—4 rims; 1 base; 13 sherds.

315 Rim, smooth cream-buff external surface. Some yellow glaze on interior.

316 Rim, yellow lead glaze on interior.

317 Miniature olive jar. Green glazed interior. Typical fabric with cream-white exterior surface.

318 Rim of unusual fine red dense fabric with a clear green-yellow lead glaze on the interior. The exterior surface is white-cream with large patches of green glaze.

STARRED COSTRELS (Fig 37)
First half of 17th century

These vessels have flat bases and a flattened body on opposite sides of the vessel. They usually have a protruding footring. A blue or yellow star is painted on the body. They are usually dated to the first half of the 17th century, although one sherd from Pleshey Castle appears to be an early 16th-century prototype. They are thought to originate in Spain in the Seville area (fig 23, pl 82, Cotter, 1958; Hurst, 1977).

Fabric: Friable chalky cream to pink fabric, very porous as inclusions have been fired out, leaving numerous cavities. Spatterings of tin glaze on external surfaces.

2 rims; 8 bases; 12 handles; 19 sherds, 16 of them with blue stars, 1 with pink star, 1 with orange star.

319 Base sherd with pink buff interior and cream coloured exterior with some very slight traces of decayed tin glaze. Abstract random scored lines occur near the base.

320 Orange fabric—unusual. Shoulder of star costrel with orange painted, eight-pointed star on decaying yellowy tin glaze. Cordon just above centre of star.

321 Typical kicked-up handle. Thumb impression at bottom. Decayed tin glaze.

322 Base of star costrel. Very slight traces of tin glaze.

COPPER LUSTRE (Fig 37)
16th to 17th century

Tin-glazed lustreware was not manufactured in Spain until *c*1171. Malaga in Andalusia was the main centre from 1238 onwards. In the mid-14th century potters migrated to Manises, near Valencia. Fifteenth and 16th century imports seem to have come from Aragon and Catalonia (Hurst, 1977).

Fabric: It is difficult to differentiate wares from different centres. but generally speaking those from Catalonia have a pink fabric and those from Valencia are white or buff. The fabric is fine and sandy.

Lugged Bowls
323 Rim sherd from bowl with scalloped lug and and semi-circular concentric design on the interior. Some external decoration.

324 Lug from bowl with scalloped edges and decorated in copper lustre. One horizontal copper lustre line on the exterior.

Small Bowls
Thick walled with a plain rim. 13 rims; 7 bases; 10 sherds.

325 Rim, very decayed lustre decoration on the interior which can only be distinguished by its iridescence.

326 Plain rim from small bowl with abstract zonal copper lustre decoration confined by plain copper bands. The exterior has horizontal copper lines.

327 Rim from small bowl with large copper lustre swirls on the interior and a copper lustre band on the exterior at the rim.

328 Thick plain rim with abstract copper lustre ?floral decoration on the interior and some decoration on the exterior.

329 Sherd from bowl with trimmed flat base and steep sides. Simple internal copper lustre decoration.

330 Flat bases with rosette decoration in copper
331 lustre.

Plates
With or without carination. 9 rims; 2 bases; 8 sherds.

332 Flaring rim from an open dish with internal floral type decoration in copper lustre and external horizontal bands.

333 Flat base with internal copper lustre decoration and well-defined ridge towards the base.

THE POTTERY ILLUSTRATIONS

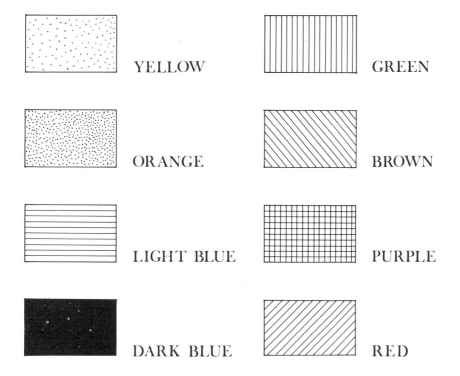

YELLOW

GREEN

ORANGE

BROWN

LIGHT BLUE

PURPLE

DARK BLUE

RED

Colour symbols used for Imported Pottery

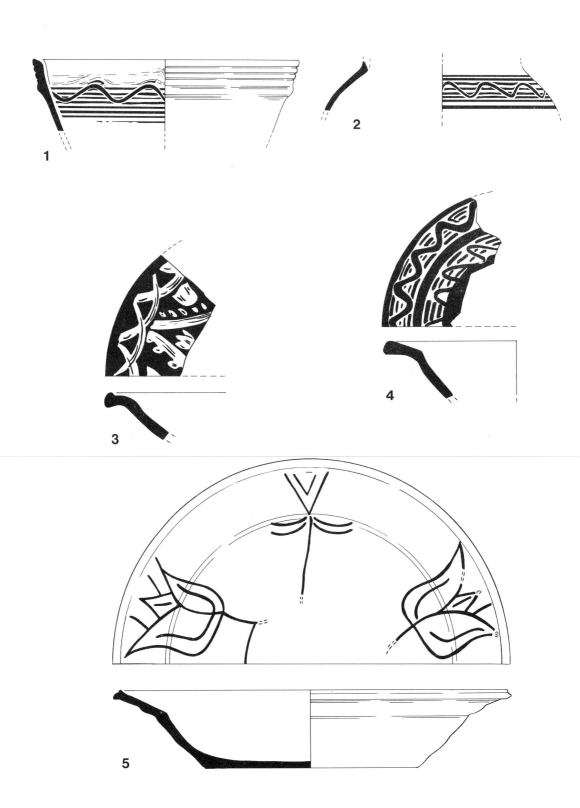

FIG 1. Britain: 1–5, Donyatt (Scale ×¼)

FIG 2. Britain: 6–12, Donyatt (Scale $\times\frac{1}{4}$)

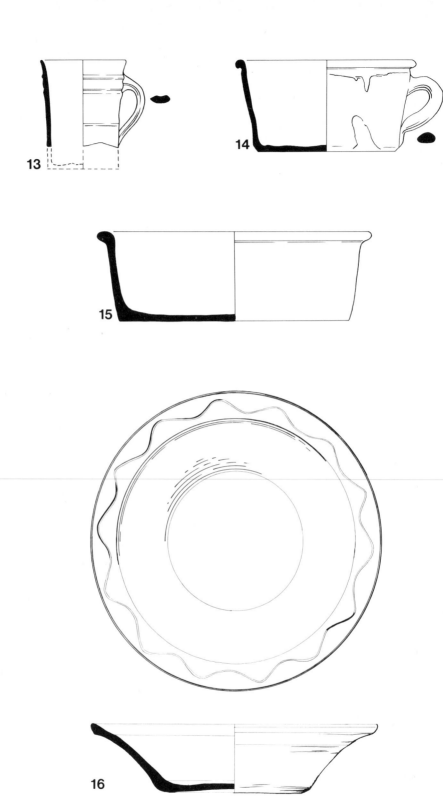

FIG 3. Britain: 13, Forest of Dean. 14–16, Hampshire (Scale ×¼)

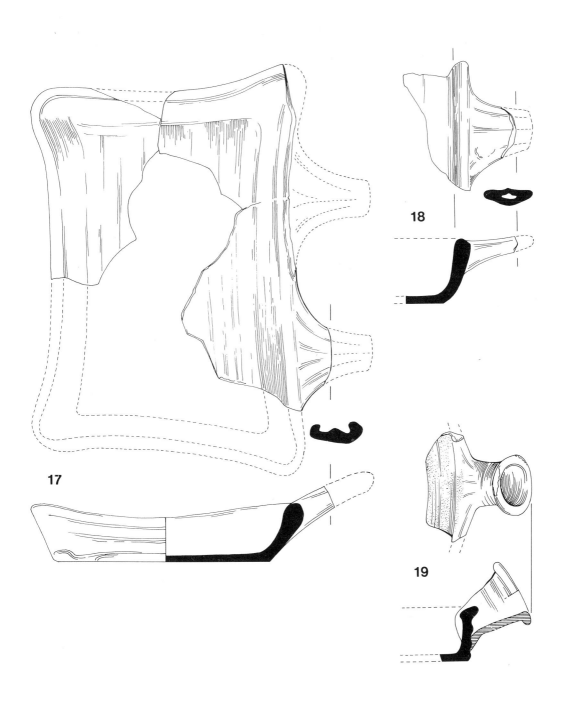

17

18

19

FIG 4. Britain: 17–19, Hampshire (Scale ×¼)

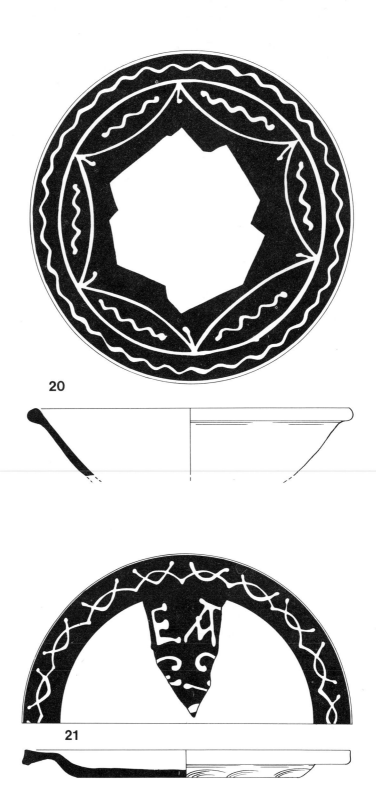

20

21

FIG 5. Britain: 20–21, Metropolitan slipware (Scale ×¼)

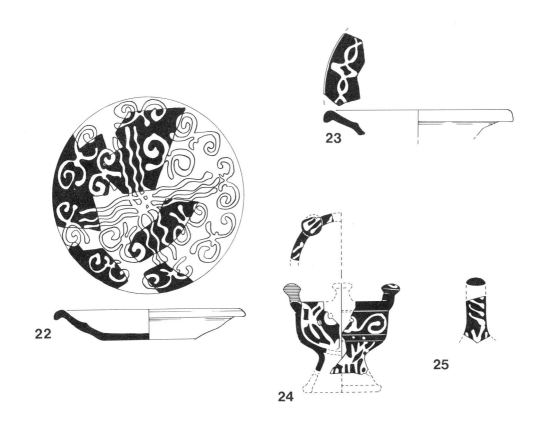

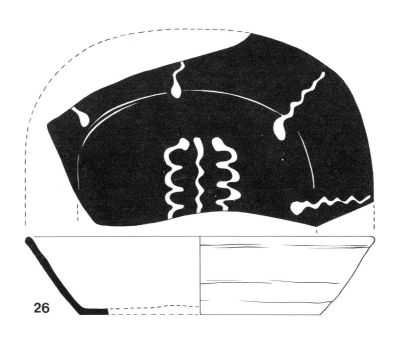

FIG 6. Britain: 22–25, Metropolitan slipware. 26, Midlands purple (Scale ×$\frac{1}{4}$)

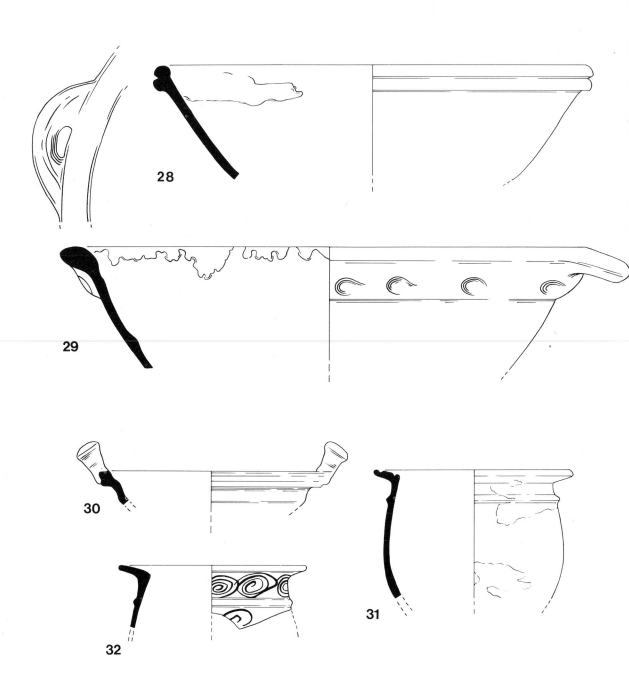

FIG 7. Britain: 27–31, North Devon (Scale ×¼)

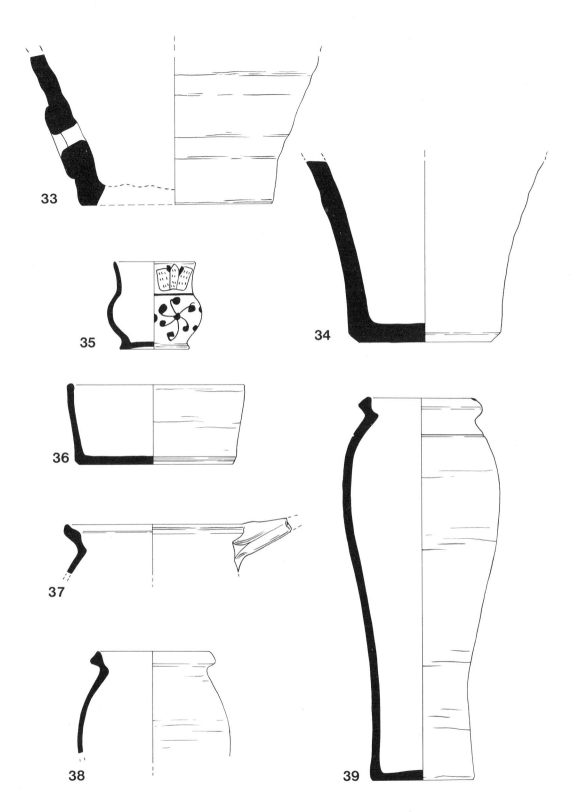

FIG 8. Britain: 32–39, North Devon (Scale ×¼)

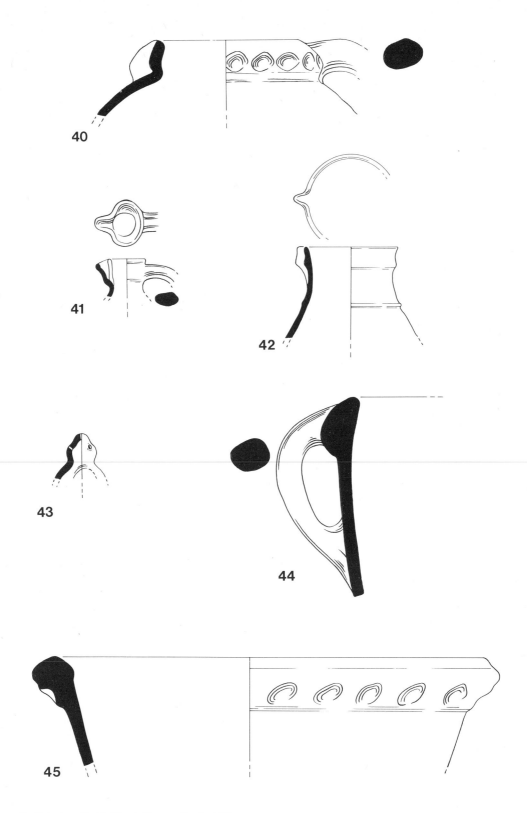

FIG 9. Britain: 40–45, North Devon (Scale ×¼)

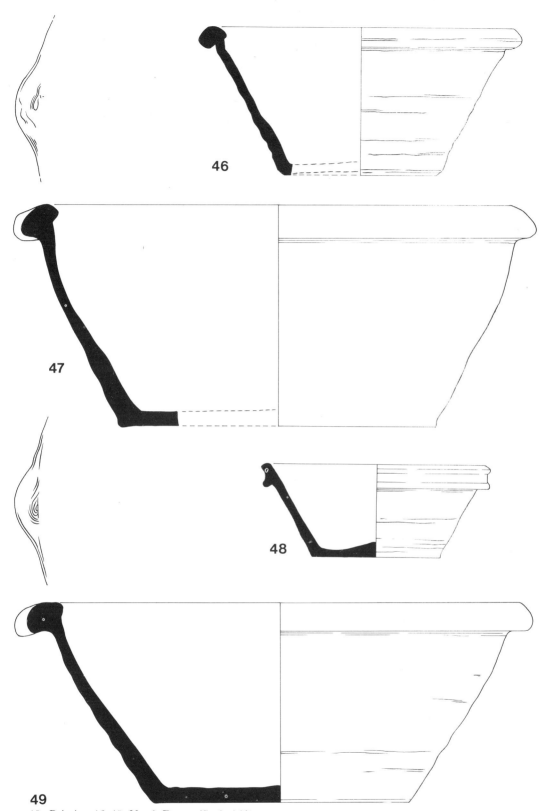

FIG 10. Britain: 46–49, North Devon (Scale ×¼)

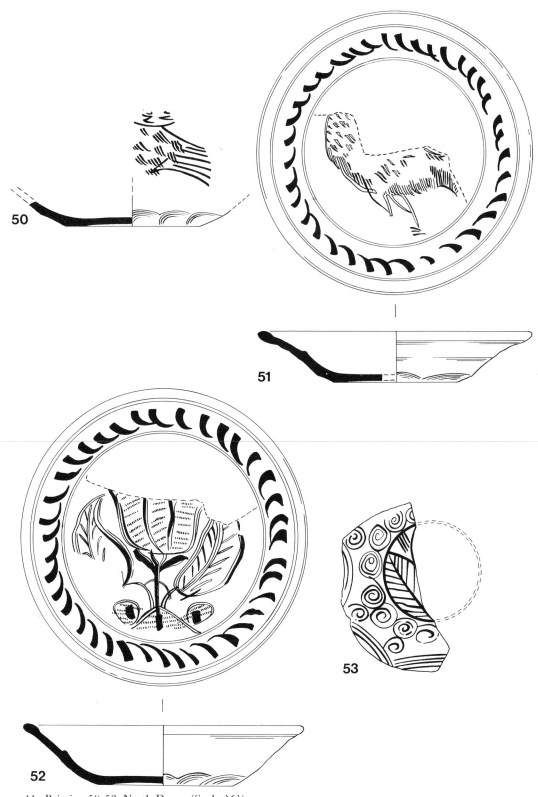

FIG 11. Britain: 50–53, North Devon (Scale ×¼)

62

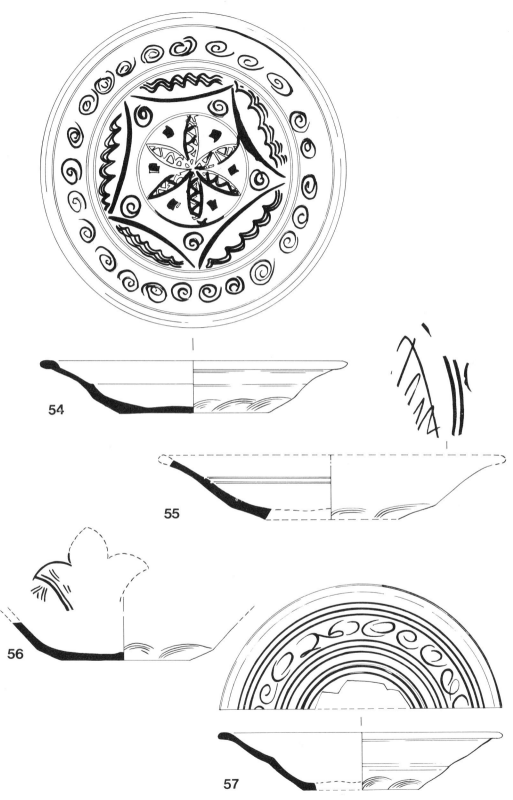

FIG 12. Britain: 54–57, North Devon (Scale ×¼)

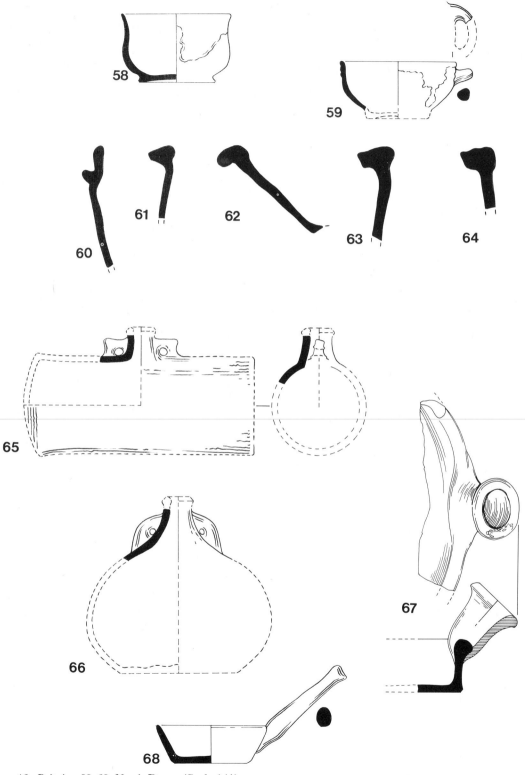

FIG 13. Britain: 58–68, North Devon (Scale ×¼)

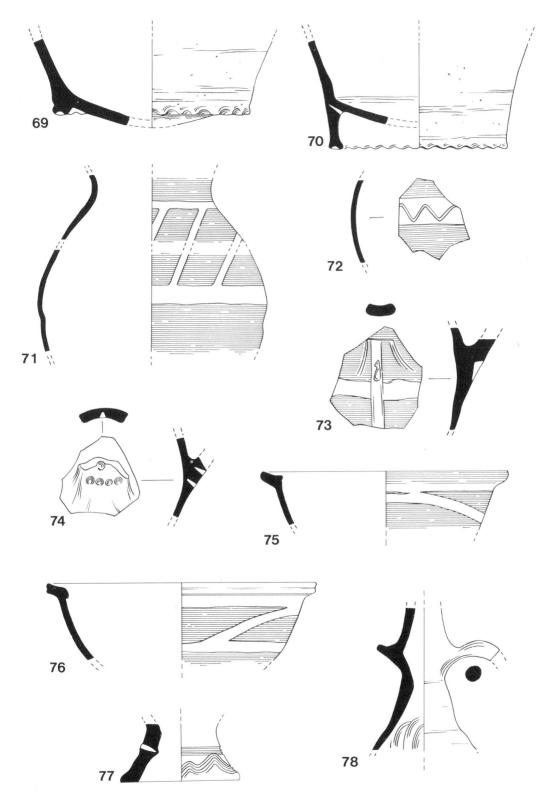

FIG 14. Britain: 69–78, South West Micaceous (Scale ×¼)

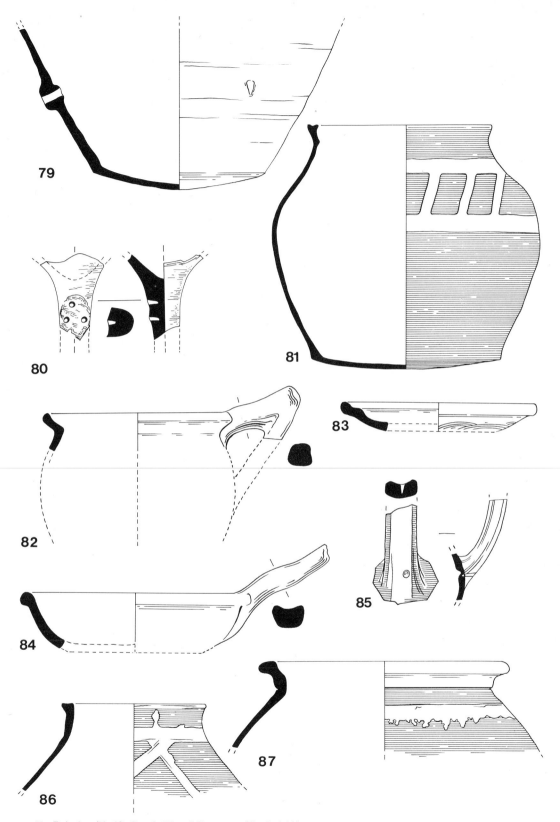

FIG 15. Britain: 79–87, South West Micaceous (Scale ×¼)

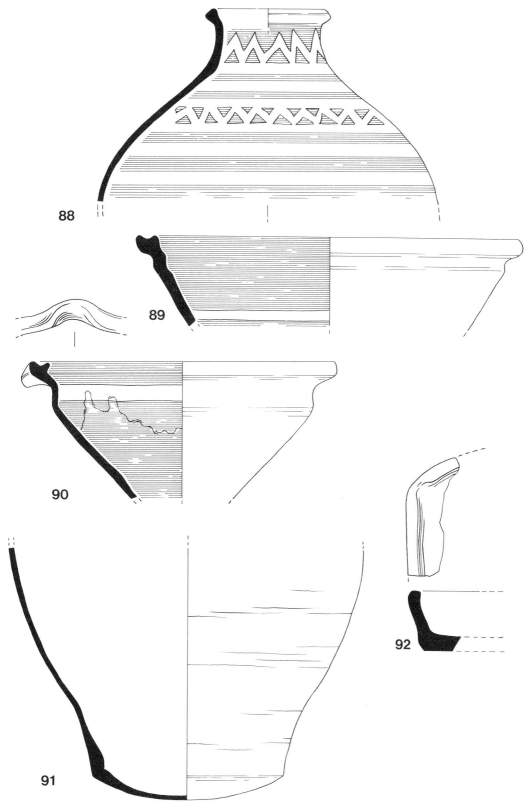

88

89

90

91

92

FIG 16. Britain: 88–92, South West Micaceous (Scale ×¼)

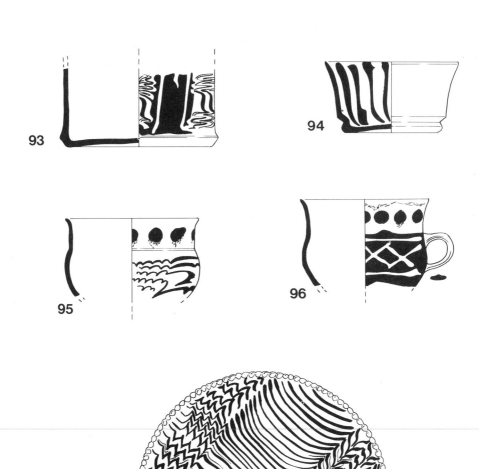

FIG 17. Britain: 93–98, Staffordshire/Bristol slipware (Scale ×¼)

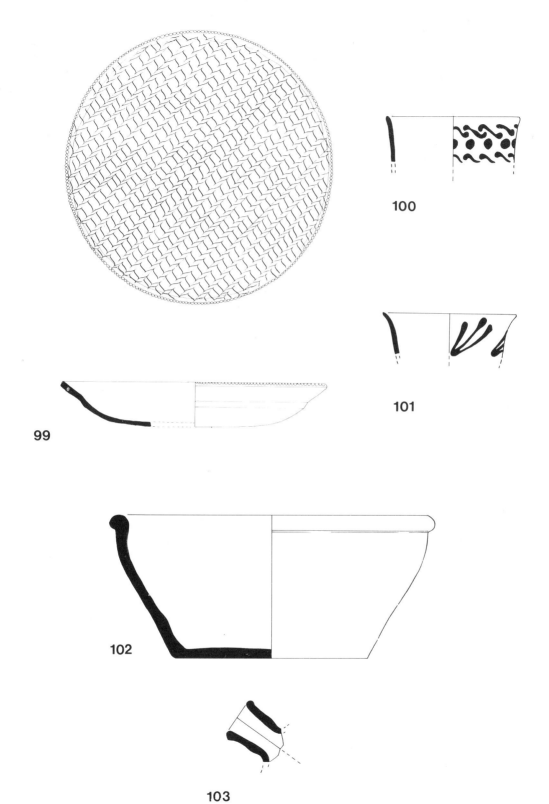

99

100

101

102

103

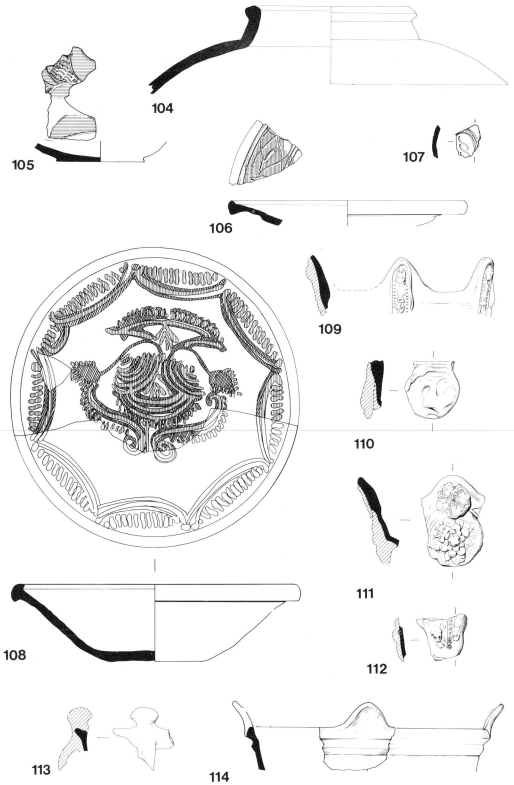

104

105

107

106

109

110

111

112

108

113

114

FIG 19. Far East: 104, Martabani. France: 105–107, Beauvais. 108, Martincamp. 109–114, Saintonge (Scale ×¼)

70

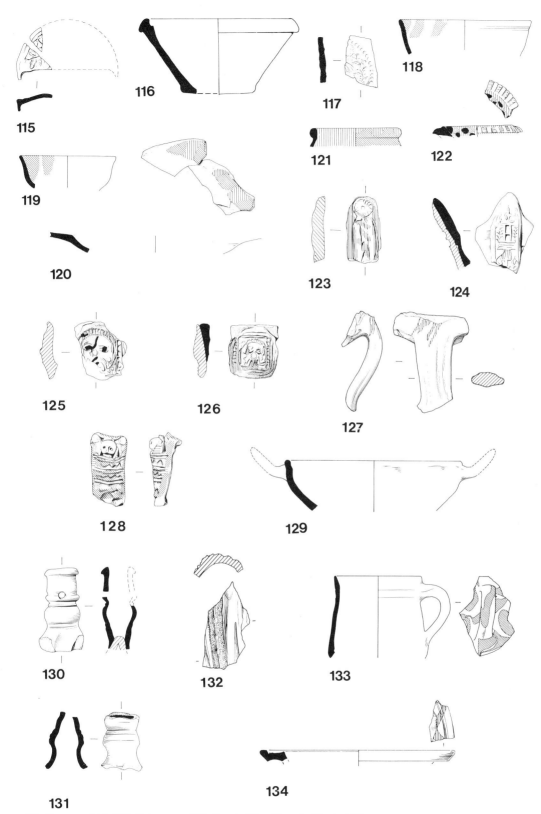

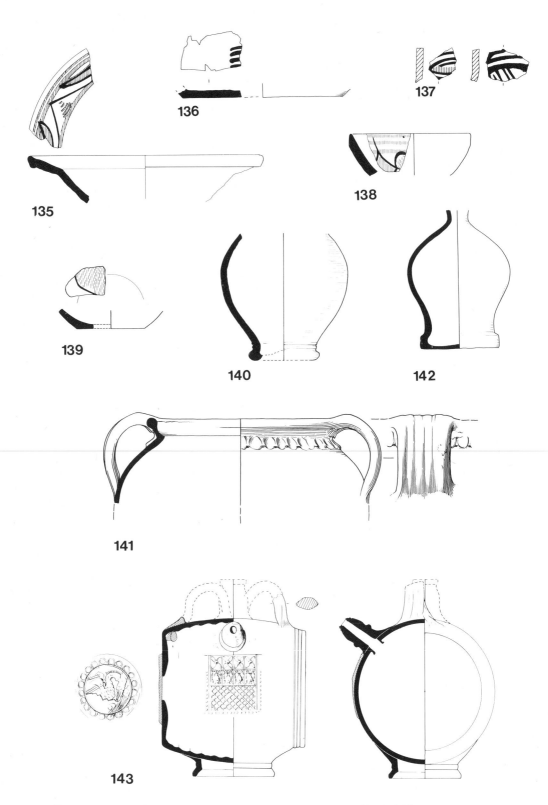

135

136

137

138

139

140

142

141

143

FIG 21. France: 135–140, South West French. 141–143, Miscellaneous (Scale ×¼)

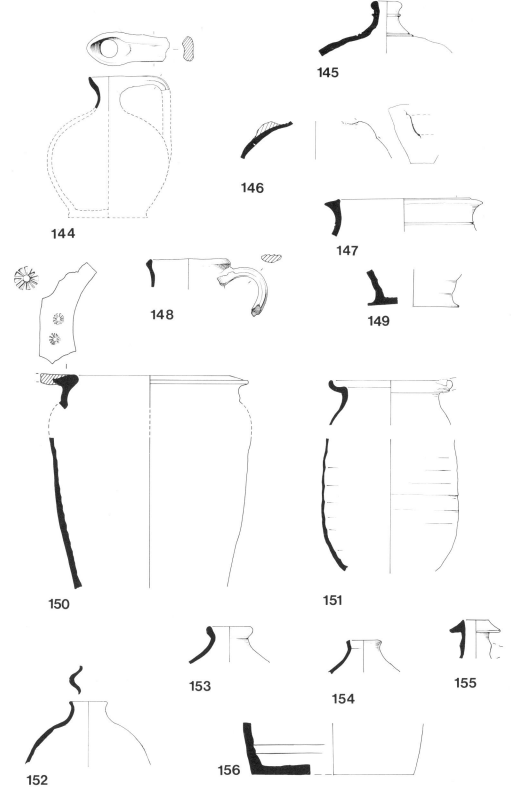

FIG 22. France: 144, Miscellaneous. 145–149, Beauvais stoneware. 150–156, Normandy
stoneware (Scale ×¼)

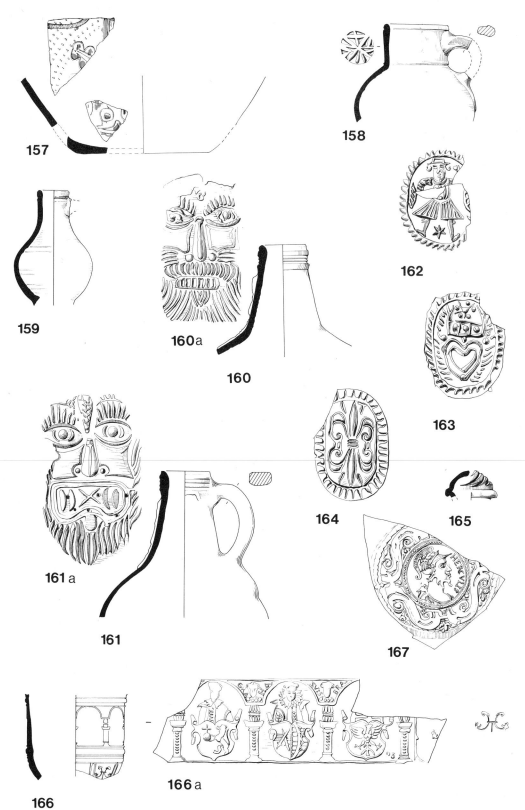

FIG 23. Germany: 157, Niederrheinische. 158 164, Cologne-Frechen. 165–166, Raeren, 167, Siegburg (Scales 160a, 161a, 162, 163, 164, 166a, 167, ×½. All others ×¼)

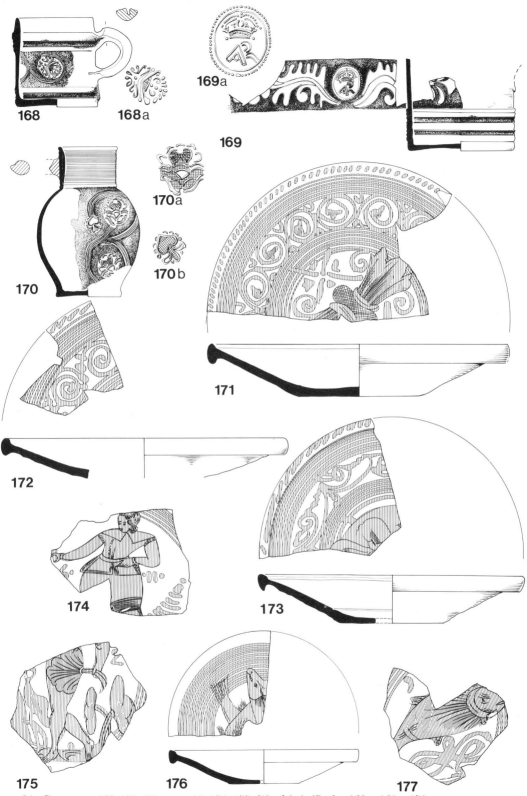

FIG 24. Germany: 168–170, Westerwald. 171–177, Wanfried. (Scales 168a, 169a, 170a, 170b, $\times\frac{1}{2}$. All others $\times\frac{1}{4}$)

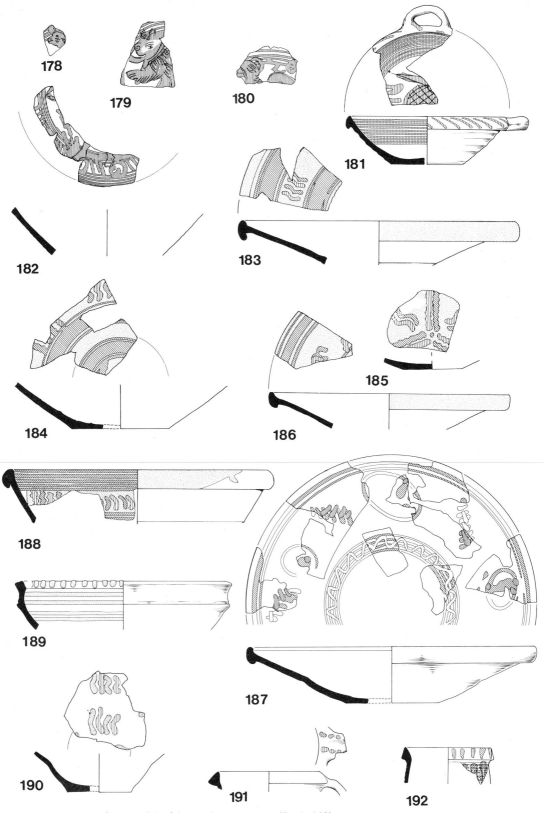

FIG 25. Germany: 178–182, Wanfried. 183–192, Weser (Scale ×¼)

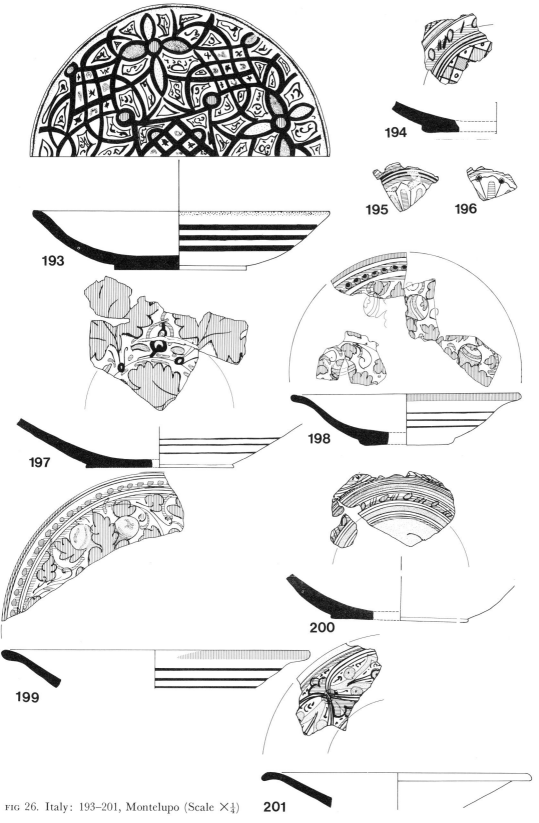

FIG 26. Italy: 193–201, Montelupo (Scale ×¼)

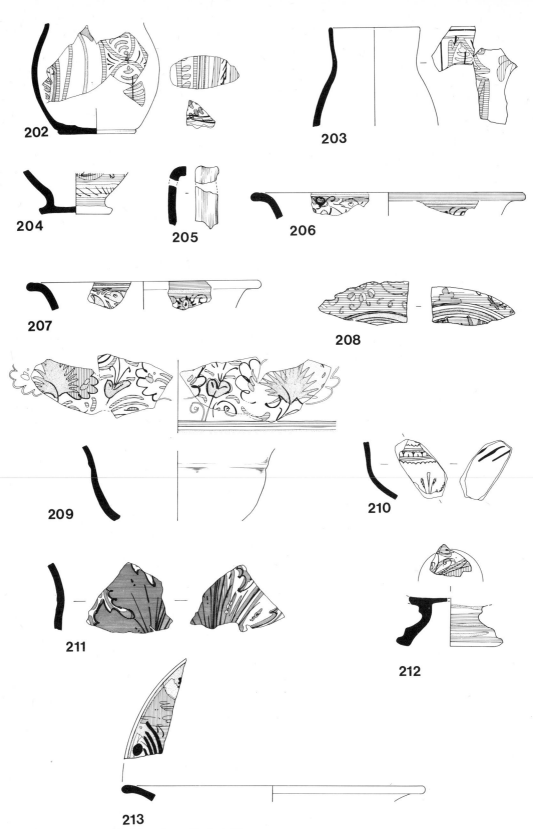

FIG 27. Italy: 202–213, Montelupo (Scale ×¼)

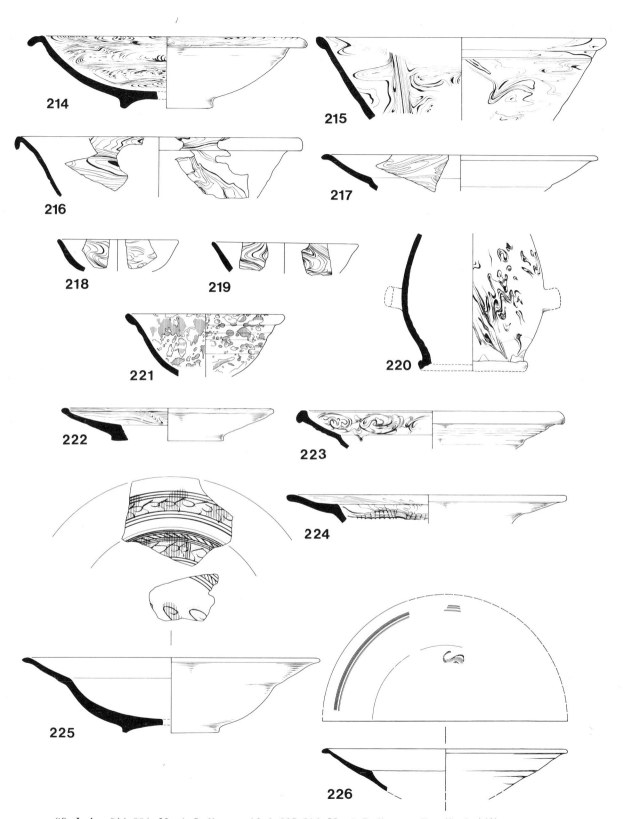

FIG 28. Italy: 214–224, North Italian marbled. 225–226, North Italian sgraffito (Scale ×¼)

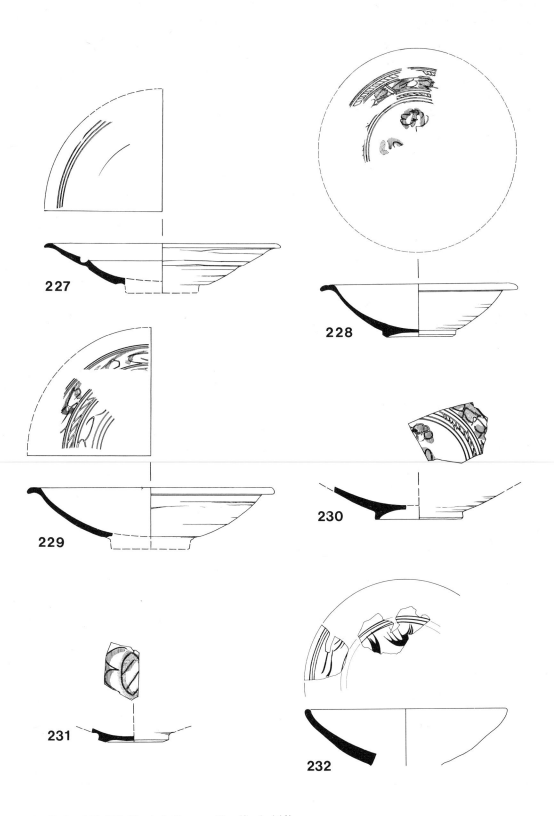

FIG 29. Italy: 227–232, North Italian sgraffito (Scale ×¼)

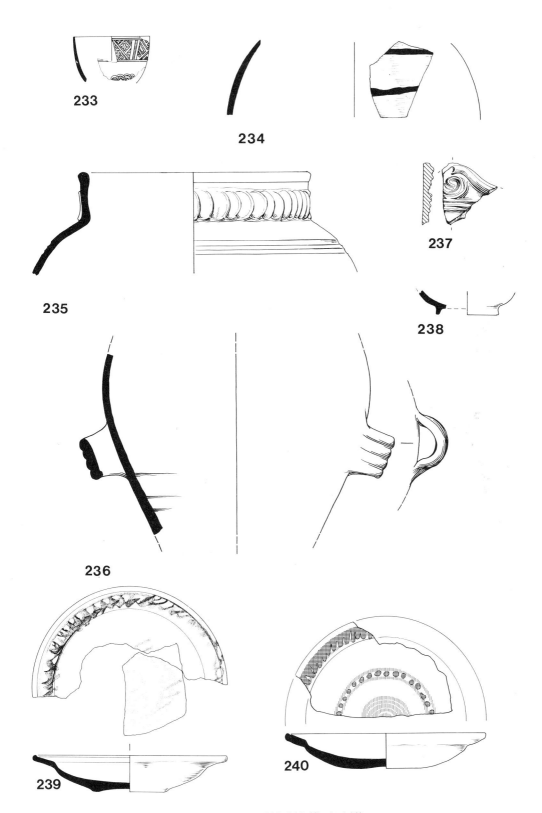

FIG 30. Middle East: 233, Persia. Mediterranean: 234–240 (Scale ×¼)

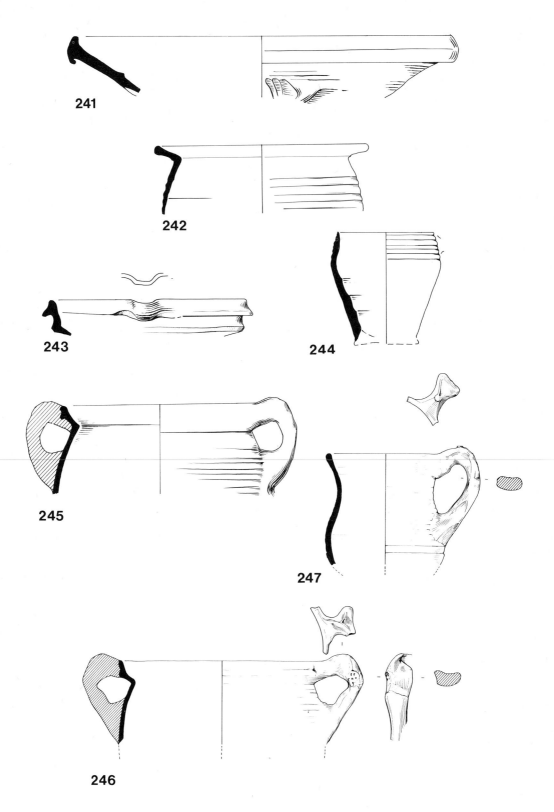

FIG 31. Netherlands: 241–245, Dutch type brown. 246–247, Dutch type, green and yellow (Scale ×¼)

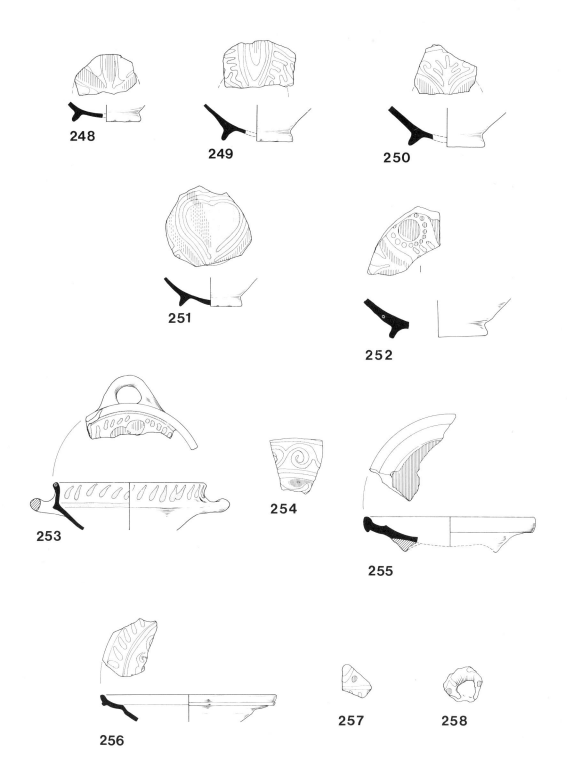

248

249

250

251

252

253

254

255

256

257

258

FIG 32. Netherlands: 248–258, North Holland slipware (Scale $\times\frac{1}{4}$)

83

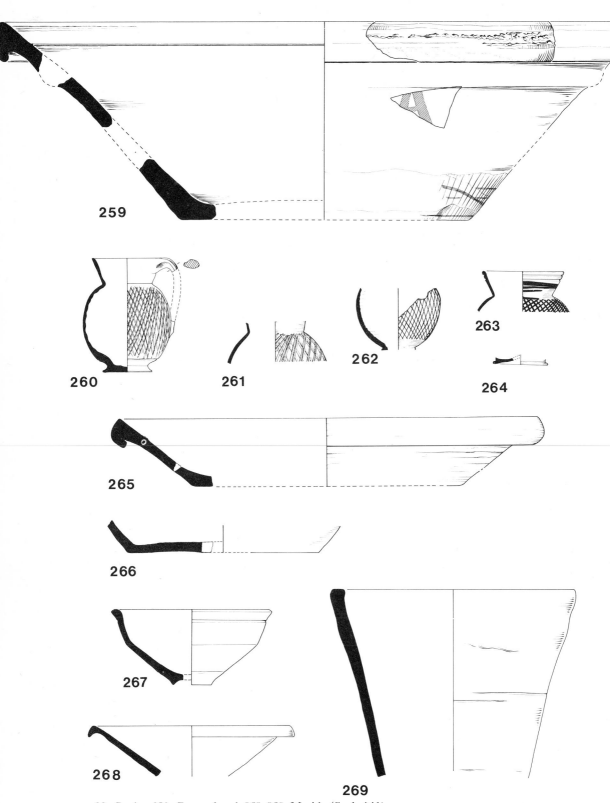

FIG 33. Spain: 259, Green glazed. 262–269, Merida (Scale ×¼)

84

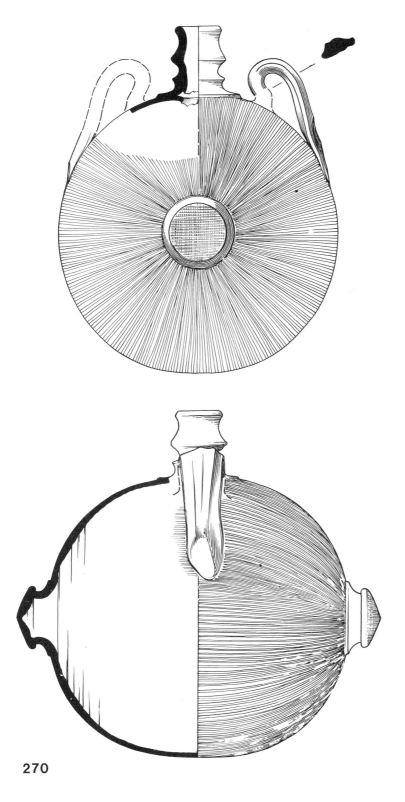

270

FIG 34. Spain: 270, Merida (Scale ×$\frac{1}{4}$)

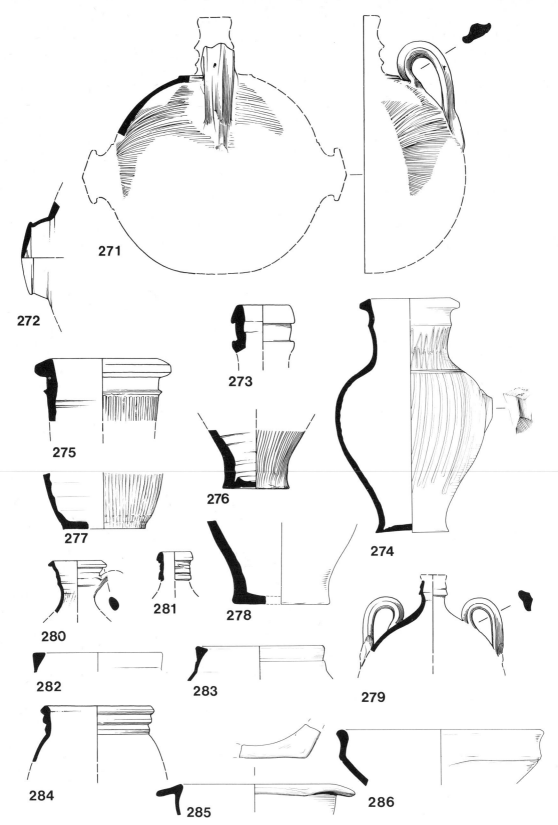

FIG 35. Spain: 271–286, Merida (Scale ×¼)

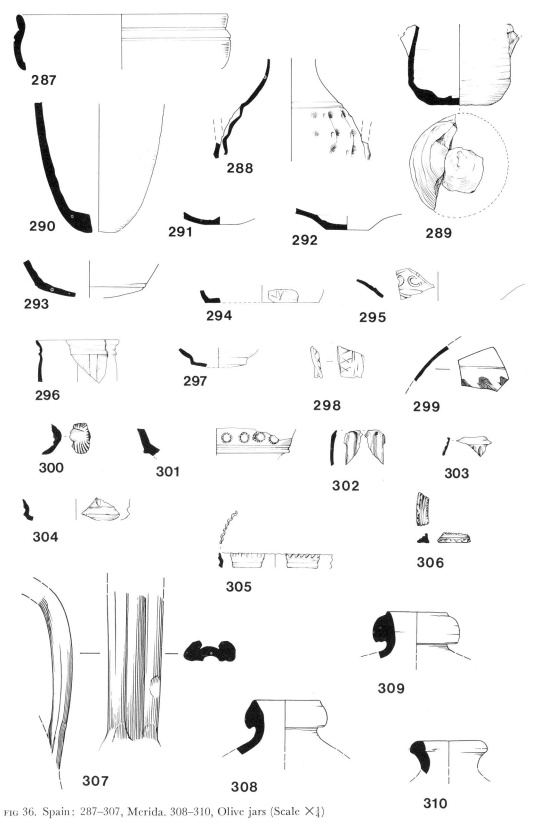

FIG 36. Spain: 287–307, Merida. 308–310, Olive jars (Scale ×¼)

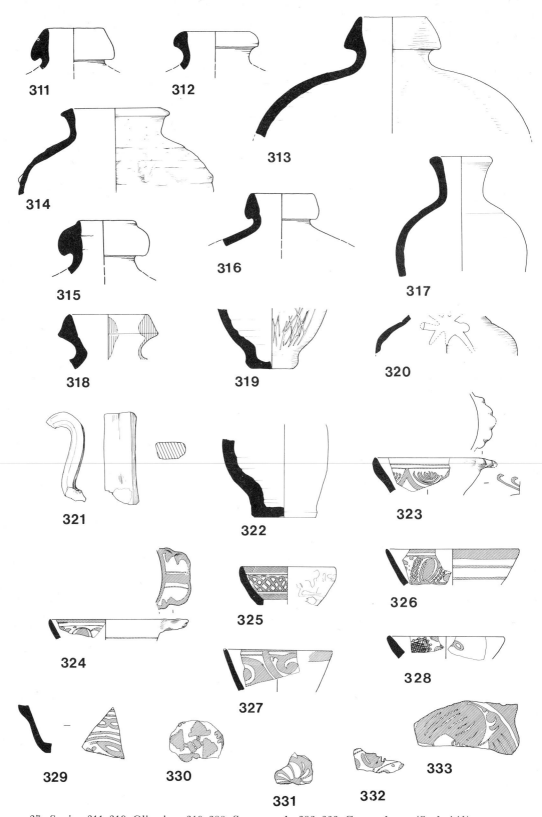

FIG 37. Spain: 311–318, Olive jars. 319–322, Star costrels. 323–333, Copper lustre (Scale ×¼)

GLOSSARY OF POTTERY TERMS

Note: This glossary is not intended to be comprehensive, but only to be used to explain or enlarge the catalogue; it does, however, underline the need for greater co-operation between potters, industrial and craft specialists, and archaeologists.

Acanthus: 'Herbaceous plant (in English also called Bear's Breech or brank-ursine), the formalised leaves of which were much used as an enrichment of mouldings and surfaces and on capitals of Corinthian and Composite Orders in Greek and Roman architecture.' (Osborne, 1971, p.1). The acanthus leaf was also used extensively as a decorative motif on German stoneware pottery (Kataloge des Kunstgewerbemuseums, Koln, 1971, nos 288, 289, 290 and others).

Agate ware: A pottery body resembling agate stone in its marbled appearance, produced by layering and mixing different coloured clays (Fournier, 1973, p 8).

Alkali: Alkali glazes can be identified visually by their icing-sugar quality which is caused by their crystalline nature derived from the use of soda or potash. These glazes were used by the potters of Western Asia and Islam, usually over a light fabric to display the distinctive colours. (Woodhouse 1974 p 77–84) Alkali glazes often craze but this gives a decorative effect. These glazes yield colour effects which cannot be obtained by other means. The beautiful vivid turquoise blues of early Egyptian pottery, and the later Iznik wares, were obtained by adding copper oxide to the glaze recipe, whilst black pigments break into greens. Remarkable sealing-wax reds can also be achieved and were often used to enhance the most usual floral designs. See Fournier, 1973, p 9 and Lomax, 1956, p 103–105 for technical information; Charleston, 1968, p 94 and Hodges, 1972, p 52 for a history. This class of pottery is a rare and exotic inclusion in British archaeological pottery assemblages, and however fragmentary is significant.

Amber glaze: A purely descriptive term intended to convey the colour of a lead glaze with between four per cent and six per cent of red iron oxide in it to make it a clear transparent yellow. It is sometimes described as a 'honey' or treacle' glaze. It was used extensively on coarse earthenwares such as Donyatt, North Devon, and early Staffordshire wares. See 'Glazes'.

Burnished: The polishing of the surface of the clay before firing, while the clay is the consistency of cheese, so that the particles of the clay are compressed. Usually used for decorative reasons, but a burnished pot can be up to fifteen per cent less porous (Fournier, 1973, p 36).

Bellarmine: Stoneware jugs and bottles made in the Frechen district of the Rhineland and decorated with a bearded mask on the neck and medallions on the body. The masks are supposed to be caricatures of Cardinal Bellarmine, although the earliest examples of bottles with medallions predate the Cardinal's career in the Church (Holmes, 1951, p 173).

Body: The material or clay from which a pot is made (Potclays, 1978). Archaeologists prefer the use of the word 'fabric'. The word can also refer to the main part of a pot.

Can Clay: Also called can marl. A clay of light buff colour found in association with coal, and used to make the early Staffordshire pottery with its characteristically light buff yellow fabric. Can clays are also found in the Bristol area at Radstock, Somerset (Rackham, 1951, p. 19–20).

Carinated: A sharp change in the angle of a pot.

Chafing Dish: 'To chafe' or 'to keep things warm by charcoal etc.' (Fowler and Fowler, 1942, p 122). A chafing dish can be made of metal or pottery. It usually consists of a dish mounted on a pedestal base which has perforations in its walls; the base of the dish may also have perforations to allow free access of air. Hot coals of charcoal are placed in the bowl: a plate containing food to be cooked is then placed on top of the dish, which may have lugs to lift the plate off the dish rim and allow circulation of the hot air. Chafing dishes were made in the Donyatt potteries and in North Devon. More ornate ones were made in the Saintonge, France. For recipes for chafing see Mrs Beeton, 1912.

Chalky: A purely descriptive term used to convey the pale tone of a fabric, not meant to infer the presence of calcium.

Cistern: A storage place for water or other liquid. Pottery cisterns are usually large barrel-shaped vessels, standing on end, the top having a large opening to receive the liquid, which may be corked after filling. The vessel is emptied by means of a tap or spigot about 2 cm from the base to allow the sediment to settle. Usually made of coarse earthenware. Good examples exist from Donyatt and North Devon and elsewhere.

Clay: Hydrated silicate of aluminium. $AL_2O_3 2SiO_2 2H_2O$. Clay is a mixture of several substances. Alumina silicate is the chief ingredient, but impurities are often present which affect the working properties, making it suitable for earthenware, stoneware, or refractory manufacture. Some impurities are harmful, such as iron pyrites and lime, which blow up in the kiln. Mica may not be particularly harmful in earthenwares but it will cause unsightly discolouration in white wares. The varying impurities give clays a wide variation in colour, from pure white through pale yellow to ochre, red and brown; grey and black are usually caused by the presence of organic material. The two essential properties of clay are that (a) when it is moist it is plastic and (b) when subjected to heat it becomes hardened and changed to a ceramic material. It is the driving off of the chemically combined water at approximately 600°C that causes the irreversible change from clay to pottery. Above 600°C more and more inclusions in the clay vitrify or melt. If the clay can stand temperatures of 1000°C it will be used for earthenware; if it can retain its shape at 1200°C to 1300°C it will be used for stoneware. Some clays tend to melt at approximately 1100°C, usually because of the presence of red iron oxide that acts as a flux. The clay may, therefore, vitrify at 1100°C and yet will not fire high enough for the application of a stoneware glaze. It is therefore a 'vitrified earthenware' (Hamer 1975, p 311).

Coarse Wares: Pottery made from a coarse clay or fabric, usually referring to red earthenware. The term implies that if this ware is decorated at all the decoration will be carried out using the most primitive techniques, such as slip trailing, as opposed to tin-glazed painting or lustre, although the basic fabric may be the same.

Cobalt: A general name for a number of compounds of cobalt and oxygen which have been used as blue stains for pottery for nearly two thousand years (Hamer, 1975, p 66). Raw cobalt oxide was used to decorate the blue Delft dishes in the 17th and 18th centuries in imitation of Chinese porcelain, and by the German potters of the Westerwald.

Combed: The technique of decorating pottery with a comb. Often used to 'band' lines around a pot, create wave patterns, or to produce stab marks. To enhance the effect, a slip of contrasting colour is often painted on the pot, and the combing carried out before the pot is dry. The Donyatt potters frequently used this method, as well as combing through a dry slip. In North Devon stabbed or pecked comb dots were used.

Copper: Used in pottery to give a decorative green colour, either in a glaze or paint. Copper oxide, CuO, is normally used. When fired in an oxidising atmosphere copper oxide will give green in a lead glaze; in association with tin oxide it produces turquoise blue. When it is used in a reducing atmosphere reds are produced. When painted onto a tin glaze and fired in a reducing atmosphere it will give copper lustre effects, as seen in Spanish lustrewares. See 'Lustre'.

Core: The central part of the pot wall. This may appear as a sandwich of grey or black between two outer surfaces of red oxidised fabric. This sandwich effect is an accident of the firing process, which may be produced by two circumstances: (1) while the outer surfaces have oxidised, not all the carbon from the organic matter in the centre of the wall of the pot has burnt out because of insufficient firing; or (2) a predominantly reducing atmosphere has prevailed throughout the firing until the last stages, when the fires have died down, allowing free oxygen to enter the kiln and oxidise only the outer surfaces of the ware.

Costrel: A vessel of barrel or bottle shape, usually with two handles or lugs on each side of a small spout. The smaller ones were used by field labourers for drinking during harvest.

Cresset Lamp: Usually with a shallow bowl for oil and a pointed base to fit into an iron ring. An ancient form which became common in Britain in the medieval period (Charleston, 1968, p 11, fig 325; Cunliffe, 1964, p 105.

Delft: The centre in the Netherlands which became famous for its tin glazed products which then became known as Delft ware. See 'Tin Glaze'.

Divided Dish: A large dish with a built-in clay division across the middle to give it two compartments. Made in the Midlands and West Country (Brears, 1974, opp p 124).

Earthenware: Pottery made of a porous fabric, fired between 600°C and 1100°C. If the fabric becomes vitreous below 1100°C it is a vitrified earthenware. See 'Vitrified'. Many clays can be fired at earthenware and stoneware temperatures. Earthenwares tend to be red in colour because the addition of iron through geological processes lowers the temperature range, making it distort or melt at much above 1100°C. Earthenwares included in the catalogue are as follows: Beauvais Sgraffito ware; Donyatt pottery; Hampshire ware; Italian maiolica ware; Metropolitan slipware; Midlands Purple ware; North Devon pottery; North Holland slipware; North Italian Sgraffito and Marbled wares; Saintonge pottery; Spanish olive jars and tin-glazed lustrewares; Staffordshire/Bristol wares; South West Micaceous ware; Sussex pottery; Wanfried ware; Weser ware. *Note:* lead glazes can only be used on earthenware: they volatilise above 1100°C.

Fabric: Ceramic material from which the pot is made. See 'Body'.

Faience: Faience was the term originally given to wares from Faenza in Northern Italy. These were tin glazed wares of the majolica type (Hamer, 1975, p 117.) Faience is now taken to mean the tin glazed wares of France. See 'Tin Glaze'.

Feathering: This is a particularly confusing term as it is used to describe a large range of decorative motifs. It can be used to describe the decorative motif of painted feathers, in groups or scattered, used notably on Worcester porcelain *c*1807–18, and also at Minton. It can also describe the moulded border on the scalloped rim of plates. However, in archaeological catalogues of the post-medieval period, 'feathering' or 'feather pattern' is usually applied to the decorative effect of dragging a thin brush or feather through dissimilar slips while they are still wet, thus creating a 'feathered' or marbled decoration (Lewis, 1969, p 32, fig 49; Hamer, 1975, p 117).

Firing: The process of conversion from clay to pot. It involves heat of at least 600°C (1112°F). See 'Clay' (Hamer, 1975, p 121–5).

Flaked: Pottery sometimes becomes flaked by frost, but most often it is caused because of the difference of the coefficient of expansion between the fabric, slip and glaze. This is particularly true of Donyatt pottery. Tin glazes are also subject to flaking and 'crawling' due to the same reason.

Flange: A projecting flat rim, collar or rib.

Flint: Cryptocrystalline native silica. SiO_2. Flint is almost pure silica. Used to harden fabrics of bone china, porcelain, and some white earthenwares, it may also be used in lead glazes to render them insoluble in water and prevent lead poisoning; flint dust, however, is a health hazard in itself. Flint inclusions are often seen as white calcined dots in various fabrics, but it was not added intentionally before the Industrial Revolution.

Fluting: Shallow parallel grooves running vertically on the shaft of a column, pilaster or pot (Fleming and Honour, 1977, p 298).

Glaze: A vitreous coating, usually silica, applied to a porous body to seal it against penetration of liquids, and usually to give it a smooth and brilliant surface. The silica of many glazes is derived from the ceramic body itself. It requires a flux or modifier: lead oxide is the one most commonly used in the earthenware temperature range. Above 1100°C lead starts to volatilise. Lead glazes can be oxidised or reduced, and can be coloured using oxides. Seven per cent tin oxide makes a clear transparent lead glaze become a white opaque glaze which will cover up an inferior body. 'Tin Glaze' is, in fact, lead glaze stained white, in the same way that an amber glaze is a lead glaze stained amber by the addition of iron oxide. Salt glaze is the name given to all glazes achieved by volatilising common salt (sodium chloride) inside the kiln. See 'Salt Glaze'. Alkali glazes were not produced in Europe but were the speciality of the workshops of Iznik, Western Anatolia. Some alkali glazed sherds have been found in Plymouth excavations. See 'Alkali'.

Gravel: Coarse sand and small stones. Sometimes found in clays as unwanted inclusions, but sometimes added to clays to open up the texture to help them withstand the thermal shock of uneven firing, or use in the course of daily cooking. Potters call the intentional addition of sands or gravel 'grog' while archaeologists call it 'tempering'. See 'Grog'. The addition of grog was practised in the North Devon potteries which added river gravel to their clay. This practice is described by W Fishley Holland who was one of the last of the true North Devon potters (Fishley Holland, 1958, p 11).

Grog: Usually ground fired body, sand, or gravel added to the clay to provide texture, both tactile and visual, along with bite for better control in forming. Grog is an opener which helps the clay to dry uniformly. It cuts down overall shrinkage and hence any tendency to crack or warp. Archaeologists call this practice tempering, but this is quite another practice in the Potteries where tempering is the addition of water to clay powder (Fournier, 1973, p 226).

Inclusions: Matter that is not part of the fabric but included as grog intentionally, or impurities accidentally. Often useful for identification purposes.

Iridescent: Exhibiting changing colours like those of the rainbow, noted on Spanish lustreware, but also seen on old pottery and glass due to the refraction of light through the micro-flaking.

Iron: Iron oxides, FeO, Fe_2O_3, Fe_3O_4, are the commonest colourants in individual pottery, usually giving yellows, browns, blacks, and greys. Known by both their English names and their chemical names, e.g. red iron oxide is Ferric oxide. Fe_2O_3. The oxide responds differently to different glazes and kiln atmospheres. There are many forms of iron that are useful, but it can be an unwanted impurity in the form of iron pyrites, an ore of iron and sulphur which forms gases in the clay, cracking or blowing it up (Hamer, 1975, p 159–165). See also the effect of different atmospheres on iron under 'Reduction'.

Kiln: Furnace or oven. Essentially a container of refractory clay into or around which heat is introduced, either by combustion or by radiant heat. A kiln must be capable of reaching at least 600°C. A wide range of kiln types was in use in the medieval and early post-medieval periods (Hodges, 1964, p 35).

Knife Jabbed: Jabbing pottery handles with a knife was a common practice on medieval pottery. It helped the thick handle dry out a little faster, and therefore not crack away from the notably thinly thrown jugs. Knife jabbing can be seen in St German's type products.

Knife Trimmed: The most primitive way to remove some of the unwanted thicker clay from the base of a pot. A more sophisticated method is to invert the pot and 'turn' off the thickness. This process is also known as 'fettling'.

Lead: A heavy, soft, grey metal. Lead oxide, PbO (ashes of lead) and lead sulphide, PbS (galena) are widely distributed, and were thus available to early potters. First used in Britain by the Romans (Grimes, 1930). Lead was not used extensively until medieval times. All raw lead glazes are extremely poisonous, even after firing.

Lip: The pouring device either pressed (pulled) out of the pot rim itself, or modelled separately and applied to the pot before it is fired.

Lug: A small handle or pierced piece of clay on the side of a pot; a rudimentary handle.

Lustre: A thin metallic surface on a glaze. The pure metal is deposited on the glaze surface by many different methods, but all involved a reduction from an oxide or a resinate to the pure metal. The metals used are gold, silver, platinum, copper, bismuth and tin. The Spanish lustres were copper lustres, often with some silver. The rich lustre was often mistaken for gold (Hamer, 1975, p 187; Fournier, 1973, p 173; Frothingham, 1951).

Maiolica: May be spelled Majolica. Italian decorated tin glazed wares. See 'Tin Glaze'.

Manganese: A metallic element, oxide Mg, used as a colouring agent, typically brown or purple-brown (Fournier, 1973, p 145–6; Hamer, 1975, p 193–5).

Marbling: The incomplete mixing of two or more slips of different colours or tones on the surface of a pot while they are liquid. It can easily be confused with Agate Ware, which is produced by the incomplete mixing of different coloured fabrics in the plastic state before firing. Marbling is a coating on the surface, while agate is right through the wall of the pot.

Mica: A general term for a group of minerals composed of hydrated silicates of alumina, with other silicates, e.g. of the alkalis. The characteristic mineral of schists, and the glittering crystals or scales in granite. The distinguishing feature of Merida red pottery, but also very noticeable in St German's type pottery. Fabrics that display mica inclusions are known as micaceous.

Mould: Any form, over or in which clay can be shaped. Usually made of pottery, plaster of paris, or metal, for pottery purposes. Staffordshire dishes were pressed over moulds, while Bellarmine masks and medallions were pressed into moulds and then applied to the pot. Moulds are much used for forming pottery in industry.

Omphalos: A boss or conical projection.

On-glaze: Decoration can be achieved in three ways: (1) by effecting it before the glaze is applied, as in slipware, thus it is under-glaze; (2) by effecting it before the applied glaze has been fired, therefore staining the actual glaze, as in tin glazed painting of Delft; or (3) by enamelling or painting on lustre after the glaze has been fired and requiring a further firing to harden on the decoration, which is known as on-glaze decoration.

Oxide: Compound of oxygen with an element or organic radical.

Oxidised: Used to describe the red fabrics of pottery fired in a kiln with a dry atmosphere and a good draught, so that a surplus of oxygen exists in the kiln. This enables all the carbon in both the fuel and the ware to be burnt out. See also 'Reduction'.

Pancheon: A large vessel wider at the mouth than the base and needing two hands to lift it. Used for settling liquids, separating fats and in the 19th century as wash bowls.

Pie Crust: Descriptive term used to describe a series of indentations to give a decorative effect to a rim, similar to pastry edges. Used by the Staffordshire and Donyatt potters and others.

Pinched: To nip with finger and thumb, which can result in a decorative finish to handles. 'Pinched pot' refers to the most primitive method of making a pot, by pinching a ball of clay with the thumb inside and the finger outside to produce a small pot.

Pipkin: A three legged pan with a straight handle.

Polychrome: Many coloured. This term may truthfully be applied to all the decorated tin glazed wares employing more than one colour. It is equally applicable to enamelled wares. It has come to be associated with the medieval decorated products of the Saintonge area (Dunning, 1933, p 94–138; Platt and Coleman-Smith, 1975).

Porous: The ability of a fired body to absorb water by capillary action. One of the main reasons for glazing earthenwares is to counteract porosity.

Porringer: A small basin used for soup or porridge.

Posset Cup: A one or two-handled cup for a drink composed of hot milk laced with ale and spices.

Pottery: Fired clay vessels. The term is narrower in its application than ceramics, as it implies only the making of pots, rather than all objects of fired clay.

Pulled: A pulled lip or handle. By subjecting the clay to a motive force of the hand or fingers a rim may be pulled into a lip while still plastic, or a lump of clay pulled into a handle.

Reduction: The extraction of oxygen atoms from oxides. Reduction is generally considered to be the result of starving the fuel of oxygen during the firing of pottery, creating carbon monoxide and hydrocarbon gases. The most startling colour changes in reduction are those of the iron and copper oxides. More subtle alterations take place in other oxides, in the glaze quality, and in fabrics. Iron oxide, Fe_2O_3, subjected to an oxidising atmosphere, becomes Ferric Oxide (red). In a reduction firing it becomes Ferrous Oxide (black). Iron in a glaze under oxidising conditions will give yellows, browns, and blacks, depending on the percentage present. The same glaze under reduction will turn green as seen in the Chinese 'celadon' glaze. Copper in a glaze in an oxidising atmosphere will give greens to blacks; the same glaze in reduction will give reds and lustres. See 'Lustre'. Reduction is, therefore, a very important element in kiln firing (Rhodes, 1973, p 263, 270–2, 299; Fournier, 1973; Hamer, 1975, p 248).

Return Handle: Term applied to a handle that sticks straight out from a pot and then is bent back sharply to return to just below the first junction with the pot, to make reinforced saucepan-type handles.

Rod Handle: A pulled, extruded, or moulded handle of round cross-section, as opposed to a strap handle which is of a flat cross-section.

Roundel: A small disc, medallion.

Salt Glaze: The name given to all wares glazed by volatilising common salt (sodium chloride) inside the kiln. Not all clays will take salt glaze: they must be of stoneware type, maturing above 1100°C. The alumina silica ratio shows whether or not it is suitable. The fabric must contain a high proportion of free silica, as the soda, when released from the chloride, immediately and freely combines with the nearest free silica to form sodium silicate which forms the glaze. Specially designed kilns are needed, of a downdraught type. Salt glazes are the most acid resistant glazes obtainable. Because of the availability of suitable clays, salt and coal, the Germans became famous for salt glazed wares. The centres producing it were Siegburg, the Westerwald area, Cologne, Frechen, Raeren, Langerwehe and others. See maps.

Scar: Mark left on a pot's surface by its sticking to other pots in the kiln.

Sgraffito: A design scratched through a slip to show a contrasting colour. This technique was used by Donyatt and North Devon potters. Several different slips can be applied to the ware and the design scratched through to different levels, a method used on Beauvais pottery, for example. The technique originated in the Middle East.

Slip: Any clay fabric mixed with water to a smooth consistency; used to decorate unfired earthenwares, and in industrial production techniques employing moulds to produce slip cast wares (Hamer, 1975, p 275–6).

Sooted: Term used to describe the blackening on the under surface of cooking pots by the deposited soot carried in cooking fires.

Stain: Oxides are used as stains to colour slips and glazes. Only mineral stains can be used in pottery as vegetable ones fire out.

Stamp: An embossed or intaglio stamp can be used to build up a pattern on clay. Impressing is a type of stamping used extensively in Westerwald wares and others.

Stoneware: It is distinguished from earthenware by its higher firing temperature. The generally accepted minimum is 1200°C and maximum is 1350°C. Having a porosity of not more than five per cent, the higher fired stonewares may also be impermeable. Stoneware does not need either lead or boron in the glaze: indeed, lead could not be used as it would volatilise (Rhodes, 1973, p 22). Stonewares included in the catalogue are from the Westerwald area; Cologne; Frechen; Raeren; Langwehe and Siegburg.

Tempered: See 'Grog'.

Throwing: The action of making a pot on a quickly rotating wheel using only the hands and, for lubrication, water. The process involves centreing a spinning lump of plastic clay upon the wheel-head. When the clay is running true or is 'centred' it is opened in the centre, an inside base is formed, and the walls of the pot are lifted from the remainder of the clay by a series of upward movements involving the balanced pressure of the fingers inside and outside the pot. Throwing remained the principal method of repetition manufacture from the development of early civilisation till the onset of the Industrial Revolution. Throwing rings, horizontal ridges, are evident on most thrown pots.

Thumbed: See 'Pinched'.

Tin Glaze: Tin oxide, SnO_2, is insoluble. Tin is the most important and efficient opacifier. Zinc oxide, ZnO, can be used but twice as much is required to opacify the same amount of glaze. Six per cent tin oxide is usually used to make a lead glaze a suitable white for painting on with cobalt blue or manganese purple; much in excess of this amount causes pin holing and crawling. The term tin glaze is a descriptive term to describe a lead glaze which has been opacified in this way. Delfts, faiences and maiolicas are tin glazes, as are the underlying glazes of the Spanish lustre-wares.

Transverse Handle: A horizontal handle; found on Dutch earthenwares, German slipwares, and the products of North Devon and Donyatt and others.

Turned: The cheese-hard pot is inverted onto the wheel head, centred, and the surplus clay around the foot is carved off. The pottery can be turned horizontally on a lathe. The process is known as 'fettling' in the pottery industry.

Under-glaze: To decorate before the application of the glaze.

Vascular: Having cavities, caused by acids eating away inclusions when a pot is buried in the soil.

Vitrified: Vitrification, the furthest stage to which a fabric can be fired without deformation and up to its melting point. Vitrified earthenware is often confused with stoneware. Many of the Romano-British potters produced vitrified earthenware, the most notable example being from the New Forest Roman potters (Fulford, 1975, p 24).

Wedging: A hand process of preparing plastic clay which involves mixing and compressing the clay, similar to kneading. Wedging is required to render the clay a homogenous consistency throughout, to extract air, and to thoroughly mix (Hamer, 1975, p 315–16; Fournier, 1973, p. 248–50).

Wire Marks: A wire can be used to cut a thrown pot off the wheel head. This wire has a hand grip at each end, similar to a cheese wire. The wire is looped around the pot and constricted, resulting in a series of spiral marks, often found on the bases of German stonewares.

Zoomorphic: Pertaining to or exhibiting animal forms; representing animals.

BIBLIOGRAPHY

Baart, *et al.* (1977) *Opravingen in Amsterdam*

Barber, J and Oswald, A (1969) Marked Clay Pipes from Plymouth, Devon, *Post-Medieval Archaeol*, 3, 122–42

Barton, K J (1964) The Excavation of a Medieval Bastion at St Nicholas's Almshouses, King Street, Bristol, *Medieval Archeol*, 8, 184–212

Barton, K J (1975) *Pottery in England*

Barton, K J (1977) Medieval and Post-Medieval Pottery from Gorey Castle, *Annual Bulletin of the Societé Jersiase*, 22, part 2, 63–82

Beeton, Mrs (1912) *Everyday Cookery*

Bemrose, P J (1973) *English Ceramic Circle*, 9, part 1

Blockley, K (1978) Woolwich, *Post-Medieval Archaeol*, 12

Brears, P (1971) *The English Country Pottery*

Caiger-Smith, A (1973) *Tin-Glaze Pottery*

Celoria, F S C and Kelly, J H (1973) *City of Stoke-on-Trent Museum Archaeological Society Report*, no 4

Chami, E (1963) L'Art Céramique du Beauvaises, *Cahiers de la Céramique du Verre et des Arts du Feu*, 30, 79–116

Charleston, R J (1968) *World Ceramics*

Clarke, P V and Hurst, J G (1978) German Stoneware in P Schofield, Excavations south of Edinburgh High Street 1973–4, *Proc Soc Antiq Scot*, 1975–6

Coleman-Smith, R and Pearson, T (1970) *Donyatt Research Group Interim Report*

Coleman-Smith, R and Pearson, T, with Morley, I and others (forthcoming) *Excavations at the Donyatt Potteries, Somerset*

Cooper, E 1972) *A History of Pottery*

Cotter, J L (1958) Archaeological Excavations at Jamestown, Virginia, *Archaeological Research Series IV*, National Park Service, US Department of the Interior

Cox, W E (1953) *The Book of Pottery and Porcelain*, vols 1, 2

CRAAGS (forthcoming) *Committee for Rescue Archaeology in Avon, Somerset and Gloucester*

Cunliffe, B (1964) *Winchester Excavations 1949–1960*, 1

Davey, P J and Rutter, J A (1977) A Note on Continental Imports in the North-West 800–1700 A.D., *Medieval Ceramics*, I, 17–30

David, E (1977) *English Bread and Yeast Cookery*

Dawson, C (1903) Sussex Iron Work and Pottery, *Sussex Archaeological Society*, 46

Dunbar, J G and Hay, G D (1960–61) Excavations at Lour Stobo 1959–60, *Proc Soc Antiq Scot*, 94, 206

Fanning, T and Hurst, J G (1975) A mid-seventeenth century pottery group and objects from Ballyhack Castle, County Wexford, *Proc Roy Ir Acad*, 75, section C, no 6, 103–18

Fay, A (1973) La Potérie Verrisé a décor gravé sur engobe au XVIᵉ siècle, *Cahiers de la Céramique du Verre et des Arts du Feu*, 53, 37–4

Fisher, J L (1960) Harlow Pottery, *Trans Essex Archaeol Soc*, 25, part 3

Fishley Holland, W (1958) Fifty Years a Potter, *Pottery Quarterly*

Fleming, J and Honour, H (1977) *The Penguin Dictionary of Decorative Arts*

Fournier, R (1973) *Illustrated Dictionary of Practical Pottery*

Frothingham, A (1951) *Lustreware of Spain*

Fulford, M G (1975) New Forest Roman Pottery, *Brit Archaeol Rep*, 17

Göbels, K (1971) *Rheinishes Töpferhandwerk*, Frechen

Goggin, J M (1960) The Spanish Olive Jar, *Yale University Publications in Anthropology*, 62

Goggin, J M (1968) Spanish Majolica in the New World. Types of the sixteenth to eighteenth centuries, *Yale University Publications in Anthropology*, 72

Green, J N (1977) The Jact Vergulde Draek Wrecked Western Australia 1656, *Brit Archaeol Rep*, supplementary series 36 (1)

Greenfield, E (1964) Excavations of a bombed site in Chapel Street, Exeter, *Rep Trans Devonshire Ass*, 96

Grimes, W F (1930) The Works Depot of the Twentieth Legion at Castle Lyons, Holt, *Y Cymmrodor*

Haggar, R G (1950) *English Country Pottery*

Hamer, F (1975) *The Potter's Dictionary of Materials and Techniques*

Heath, A (1937) *A Handbook of Ceramic Calculations*

Hodges, H (1964) *Artifacts*

Holmes, M R (1951) The so-called Bellarmine mask on imported Rhenish stoneware, *Antiq J*, 31, 178–9

Hurst, J G (1964) Stoneware jugs: Flemish Stoneware Jug in B Cunliffe *Winchester Excavations* 142–3

Hurst, J G (1966) Imported Flasks in Kirkstall Abbey Excavations 1960–4, *Publ Thoresby Soc*, 51, no 112, 54–9

Hurst, J G (1967) The Pottery in L Keen, Excavations at Old Wardour Castle, Wiltshire, *Wiltshire Archaeol Natur Hist Mag*, 62, 67–78

Hurst, J G (1972) A Wanfried Dish from Newcastle, *Archaeol Aeliana ser 4*, 50, 259–62

Hurst, J G (1974) Sixteenth and seventeenth-century imported pottery from the Saintonge in V I Evison, H Hodges, J G Hurst (eds) *Medieval Pottery from Excavations*, 221–61

Hurst, J G, Neal, D S and Van Beuningen, H J E (1975) North Holland Slipware in J G N Renaud (ed) A Contribution to Medieval Archaeology, *Rotterdam Papers II*, 47–65

Hurst, J G (1977a) in D S Neal Kings Langley, *Medieval Archaeol*, 21, 155–57

Hurst, J G (1977b) Langerwehe stoneware of the fourteenth and fifteenth centuries in M Apted, R Gilyard-Beer and A D Saunders (eds) *Ancient Monuments and their Interpretation*, Essays presented to A J Taylor, 219–38

Hurst, J G (1977c) Spanish Pottery Imported into Medieval Britain, *Medieval Archaeol*, 21, 68–105

Kelly, J H (1969) The Hill Top Site Burslem, *City of Stoke-on-Trent Museum Archaeological Society*, Report no 3

Kendrick, T P (1959) The Verwood Pottery, *Pottery Quarterly*, vol 6, no 24

Klinge, E (ed 1972) Siegburger steinzeug, *Catalogue of the Hetjens-museum Düsseldorf*

Laslett, P (1971) *The World We Have Lost*

Lomax, A (1956) Alkaline Glazes, *Pottery Quarterly No 11*

MacDonald-Taylor, M (ed 1976) *A Dictionary of Marks*

Mainwaring Baines, J (1948) *Sussex Pottery*, new series no 17, part 1, Hastings Museum

Mead, W E (1967) *The English Medieval Feast*

Miedema, H (1974) *Martavanen*, Gemeentelijk Museum het princesshof, Leeuwarden

Morgan, F C (1956) Herefordshire Potteries, *Trans Woolhope Natur Fld Club*, 35

Moorhouse, S (1970) Finds from Basing House, Hampshire, c1540 to 1645, part 1, *Post-Medieval Archaeol*, 4, 76

Moorhouse, S (1972) Finds from Excavations in the Refectory at the Dominican Friary, Boston, *Lincolnshire Hist Archaeol*, 1, no 7, 21–53

Morisson, H (1975) Les Grès du XVe au XVIIe siècle, *Cahiers de la Céramique du Verre et des Arts du Feu*, 53, 21–27

Musty, J, Algar, D and Ewence, P (1969) *The Medieval Pottery Kilns at Laverstock, near Salisbury, Wiltshire*, Oxford for the Society of Antiquaries of London

Mynard, D C (1969) A Group of Post-Medieval Pottery from Dover Castle, *Post-Medieval Archaeol*, 3, 31–46

Naumann, J (ed 1974) *Meisterwerke hessischer Töpferkunst*

Newton, E F, Bibings, E, and Fisher, J L (1960) 17th Century pottery site at Harlow, Essex, *Trans Essex Archaeol Soc*, 25, part 3

Noël-Hume, I (1976) *A Guide to the Artifacts of Colonial America*

Osborne, H (1975) *The Oxford Companion to the Decorative Arts*

Norman, P and Reader, F W (1906) Recent Discoveries in connexion with Roman London, *Archaeologia*, ser 2, 10

Parvaux, S (1968) *La Céramique Populaire du Haut Alentejo*

Platt, C (1964) *Excavations at Dartington Hall, 1962*, London for the Royal Archaeological Institute

Platt, C and Coleman-Smith, R (1975) *Excavations in Medieval Southampton, 1953–1969*, 1 and 2

Plot, R (1686) *The Natural History of Stafford-Shire*

Potclays Catalogue (1978–79) Brickkiln Lane, Etruria, Stoke-on-Trent

Procacci, U (1973) *Ceramiche Antiche di Montelupo*, Florence

Rackham, B (1951) *Early Staffordshire Pottery*

Ralegh Radford, C A and Hallam, A D (1953) The History of Taunton Castle in the light of recent excavations, *Somerset Archaeol Natur Hist*, 98

Ralegh Radford, C A and Rogers, E H (1953) Two Local Costrels in the Museum of Torquay Natural History Society, *Proc Devon Archaeol Explor Soc*, 1–5, part 1

Reineking-von Bock, G (ed 1976) *Steinzeug Kataloge des Kunstgewerbemuseums*, Köln IV, 2 edn

Rhodes, D (1973) *Clay and Glazes for the Potter*

Rhodes, J and Coleman-Smith, R (forthcoming) The Hind Park Wood Pottery Site, *Trans Bristol Gloucestershire Archaeol Soc*

Rogère C (undated) *Les Potéries de Martincamp*

Russell, V (1957) *Medieval Archeol*, 1

Savage, G and Newman, H (1974) *An Illustrated Dictionary of Ceramics*

Scholten-Neess, M and Juttner, W (1971) *Niederrheinische Bauerntöpferei, 17–19, Jahrundert, Düsseldorf*

Shortt, H (1960) *Salisbury Museum 1860–1960, The Collections Illustrated*

Stephan, G *Coppengrave: Archäeologische Studien zum nordwestdeutshen Töpferzentrum um Duingen Hann. vom 13.bis zum 20.Jahrhundert*

Stewart, K (1975) *Cooking and Eating*

Thwaite, A (1973) The Chronology of the Bellarmine Jug, *The Connoisseur*, April, 255–62

Turner, D J and Dunbar, J G (1969–70) Breachacha Castle, Coll: Excavations and Field Survey, 1965–8, *Proc Soc Antiq Scot*, 102, 155–87

Watkins, C M ((1960) *North Devon Pottery and its Export to America in the 17th Century*, Smithsonian Institution, Washington

Wittop Koning, D A (1976) Mineraalwaterkruiken, *Antiek*, 10, 853–62

Woodhouse, C P (1974) *The World's Master Potters*

INDEX TO POTTERY TYPES